RUNAWAY

Into The Darkness /
Into The Light

RUNAWAY

Into The Darkness /
Into The Light

CHARLIE FERGUSON

ARPress
ILLUMINATING IDEAS.
EMPOWERING VOICES

ARPress
45 Dan Road Suite 5
Canton MA 02021

Hotline: 1(800) 220-7660
Fax: 1(855) 752-6001

Ordering Information:
Quantity sales. Special discounts are available on quantity purchases by corporations, associations, and others. For details, contact the publisher at the address above.

Printed in the United States of America.

ISBN-13:	Paperback	979-8-89389-839-2
	eBook	979-8-89389-843-9

Library of Congress Control Number: 2024923535

I

"**L**et's go Boy!" A hand grabbed him roughly by the shoulder, pulling him up. Larry's dad, jaws clenched, face red, obviously angry, pulled him up the aisle by the arm, right by the giggling girls, further humiliating him, and out the front door. Quickly leading him to a peach tree, he broke off a limb about three feet long. "Boy, when the preacher asks you to do something, you do it! You've been told before!"

"Please don't whip me Daddy," begged Larry. "I don't want to go up there." Arthur didn't say another word, just started hitting the back of Larry's legs with the rough peach tree limb. Larry was running in a circle with his dad holding on to his hand, trying to get away from the pain, when the humiliation and sense of betrayal he felt from his dad suddenly built to a rage! All the senseless whippings, all the verbal abuse, all the 'put downs' in front of his friends, all the harassment he had endured for over a year, came boiling to a head! Always before he had taken the whippings, but not this time! He suddenly had enough! He was past the point of reason; anger and frustration replaced any thoughts of possible consequences. With an explosive amount of energy he jerked free from his dad's hold and started running!

He was in such a rage that everything around him was a blur. He didn't see anything, didn't hear anything, just ran! He was a slim kid, tall for his 13 years, and could run like the wind; the rage made him even faster.

"You better come back here boy!" Arthur called to him, but Larry kept running. Arthur apparently didn't even think about trying to catch him.

He ran about a mile at that pace before becoming winded. The blind rage began to subside. Keeping a sharp lookout for his dad's '49 blue Ford, he slowed to a walk. He came to the city park and found a bench with a good view of anyone approaching, sat and rested—and thought about his situation. It was most definitely not where he expected to be this morning when he left for church. His thoughts drifted back to a few hours earlier, and he began to review in his mind the events of the morning leading up to here and now.

* * *

Larry awakened early. He wasn't sure about the time but he was sure it was Sunday morning. Light was coming through the curtains over the window and he glanced across the room at his eleven-year-old brother, Ernest, with whom he shared his bedroom. Ernest was still sleeping, something he seemed to have no trouble doing, with his mouth slightly open and snoring softly. Larry smiled as he slid out of bed, saying to himself, *"Sleep well, little brother."* He walked quickly down the hall to the bathroom, hurrying to get his shower before everyone else awakened and they would be trying to get into the bathroom. Quickly finishing his shower, he went back up the hall to his room and began to dress.

The alarm clock in his parent's bedroom went off with its usual loud clanging noise. Larry often wondered if they'd bought that particular clock because the alarm was so loud it woke everyone in the house. He could hear the muffled sounds of his Dad's complaining, and then the clock hit the floor. "Arthur, you're going to tear that clock up," he heard his mother, Ellen, say.

"Shut up woman," was his dad's reply. "I paid for it!" Larry heard him grunting as he got out of bed, shuffle down the hall, pause, and stick his head in their door. "I thought you'd probably be up. Did you use all the hot water again?" he growled.

"No sir, I didn't," Larry answered.

"You better not have!" Arthur said, and continued to shuffle toward the bathroom.

Larry continued to get dressed. It was Sunday morning, and he would be going to church, so he put on his dress blue pants and long sleeve white shirt, and then got out his tie with the diagonal blue and white stripes, put it around his neck, working it under his collar, and began carefully tying a knot. He noticed in the mirror Ernest was awake and watching him but didn't seem to be in any hurry to get out of bed. It was just as well since the bathroom was already occupied.

"Good morning, Brother," Larry said.

"Mmmmmf" was the sleepy reply, as Ernest turned on his side and shoved his face into the pillow.

Larry finished dressing and went into the kitchen. His mother was already cooking breakfast. She sat a bowl of steaming hot oatmeal and two pieces of toast on the table at his place. "I heard you get up earlier and get your shower, so I figured you'd be ready to eat something," she said.

"Thanks Mom," he said as he sat down at the table, added some milk and sugar to the oatmeal and began to eat. "Is Dad alright?" he cautiously asked.

"Yes, well, I guess so, but you could never tell by the way he acts." She sat down in a chair across the table from Larry, leaned toward Larry and said in a confidential tone of voice, "You know, Larry, he's a good man, but lately he just seems to be angry all the time. I don't know why.

It's like something is bothering him, but he won't talk about it with me. We'll just have to pray for him and hope he gets to feeling better soon."

Larry didn't say anything, just finished his bowl of oatmeal. He stood up and said, "Mom, I'm going to leave now and walk to church. See you there," he said, kissed her lightly on the cheek and hurried out the back door.

He was greeted by a 50-pound bundle of white fur wagging his tail from end to end! Spot, his dog, was always excited to see him, as Larry was Spot. Larry was always amazed this was the same dog as the skinny puppy he'd found in an alley almost three years before and brought home, begging real hard to keep him, making lots of promises about taking care of him. Finally his parents said "Ok."

"You better mean it when you say you'll take care of him. Otherwise he'll go to the pound," his Dad had said.

It seemed Spot was eternally grateful and was always 'Larry's dog.' Today, however, he was dressed for church and didn't want to get his clothes soiled. "Hi Spot. No, no, get down! Can't hug you today. I'm going to church. See you later." He massaged the one black ear that gave Spot his name, slipped out the back yard fence gate, and headed for church.

Larry had much rather walk the three blocks to church than endure the tension that would be present in the car with his family. It wasn't always this way. At one time the ride to church was a happy occasion. His Dad used to spend a lot of time with him, would play catch with a baseball, or maybe take him fishing, even taught him to swim. He was Larry's hero.

When Larry was about twelve something happened to change his Dad, and exactly what was still a mystery to him. There was a change in attitude, a withdrawal from any kind of social life except church, with only time for work and church. He always seemed to be irritated and angry. The change happened in a relatively short time period. That's when the whippings started. His Dad was always quick to take off his belt and administer punishment if given the slightest excuse. Larry's way of dealing with the change in his Dad was to avoid him at every opportunity.

It didn't take long to walk to church, a small white-washed concrete block building. Brother Raeburn, the pastor, had already been there and unlocked the door for early arrivals, as Larry knew he would. He realized he had a long wait but didn't mind, found his favorite seat and soon began to doze.

It seemed only a few minutes went by before people began to arrive and he awakened with a start. More people arrived for Sunday school, including his family. The Sunday School Superintendent gave a short prayer and then dismissed everyone to go to their separate classes. After their classes were over they reassembled for the morning service.

Ernest took a seat beside Larry and almost immediately Brother Raeburn started his weekly routine of trying to recruit a choir. None of the church members would commit to a weekly practice session so the church didn't have a permanent choir; hence the Sunday morning routine. Even though Sister McDougal, Larry's Sunday school teacher, had pointed out, "The part-time choir don't make the singing sound any better," Brother Raeburn felt the need to imitate what the much larger First Church, home of the District Superintendent, was doing.

"Alright folks, we need some people to sit in the choir and sing." Five or six members of the congregation stood up and ambled toward the choir loft. About forty remained seated but Brother Raeburn was unrelenting. "Now come on Brother Collins, Sister Collins. Frankie, you can sing. Larry, you and Ernest come on up here."

Usually Larry went to sit in the choir, but this morning he simply didn't feel like going. Who knows why? Maybe it was because he was thirteen, there were girls in the congregation, and his hormones were going crazy. Maybe it was because tonight a full moon would be shining. Maybe it was because the year was 1952. Who knows? Whatever the reason he didn't want to go up there. He sat in the pew, trying to be invisible, listening to the preacher do his dance. *"Why can't he just leave me alone?"* Larry wondered.

Ernest reluctantly gave in and went to sit in the choir. A couple of the girls giggled and Larry's face turned red, as he continued to stare at the back of the pew in front of him. "Come on Larry, come on up. You can sing," the preacher continued. Larry didn't budge. Then his Dad intervened.

* * *

Noise from a passing car snapped him back to the present. Thankfully it wasn't his Dad's car.

Defying the preacher and refusing to sing in the choir was new to Larry. Breaking away from his Dad and running, instead of taking the whipping, was new to him too. He had never experienced a rage like the one that came over him when his Dad started hitting him with the peach tree limb. It was as though someone else took over and controlled his body, someone he had no control over.

After sitting for about fifteen minutes his heart slowed, he caught his breath, and the beautiful Indian summer weather dried his perspiration. He felt some stinging on the back of his legs, pulled his pants legs up and looked at them, and saw the small rivulets of dried blood from where his Dad had hit him with the peach tree limb. The rage returned, but this time in a totally different way. The sight of his own blood caused his feelings to go icy cold inside and instantly he knew what he was going to do.

He stood up and started walking quickly to his home, only about eight or nine blocks away from the park, approaching cautiously as he got close. No one was home but Spot. Good! Letting himself in the back door, he went straight to the kitchen, helped himself to a piece of the traditional coconut cake sitting on the table that his mom made most every week, and hurriedly washed it down with a glass of cold milk.

Hearing a car turn into the driveway, he quickly sat the empty glass in the sink, ran to his room and scrambled under his bed.

"We'll find him! The police are looking for him too, and when we do find him he's got a date with my belt!" Arthur said as he was coming through the front door, obviously angry.

"Now Arthur, there's no need to go whipping him when he gets home. After all, it was your whipping that caused him to run away in the first place! You'll just make things worse. I think you whip him too much! He's a good boy and just don't need all that whipping!" Ellen said, as she walked into the kitchen, her frustration with Arthur showing. She instantly saw the empty milk glass and missing piece of cake but said nothing, and quickly moved away to distract Arthur's attention.

"Ellen, he's got to learn! He's gettin' to be more and more independent and I've got to stay on top of things! If I don't I'll lose control of him completely. The things Brother Huffstutler warned me about are startin' to come true!"

"Arthur, it seems to me you're just chasing him away by the way you're acting.

"And another thing! I wish we had never heard of Brother Huffstutler! Why, he never even had any children of his own but he thinks he knows all there is to raising other people's children. What makes you think he knows anything about how to raise them? I don't think he does! I think he's just a mean old grouch! Kinda weird old man too, if you ask me."

Arthur knew he was on the losing end of this argument, so he retreated into what was to him the ultimate argument. "Ellen, he's a man of God. He can quote chapter and verse to back up everything he says! And besides, Brother Raeburn wouldn't have him back every year for a revival if he didn't know what he's talking about. Now I don't want to hear any more about it! It's my responsibility and I have to do what I think is best." He moved toward their bedroom. "All this has wore me out and I'm gonna take a nap." He slammed the door shut behind him

Ellen angrily moved to the sink and started washing the empty glass, saying to herself, "*Yeah, you go ahead and hide!*" Closing her eyes, she whispered aloud, "God give me strength! I've about had it!"

Hearing all this, Larry retreated further under his bed, careful not to make a sound.

Around 10 pm a policeman came by and assured Arthur and Ellen he would keep looking. He said Larry was probably hiding at some friend's house and would come home in the morning. He soon left.

"I've got to get up early in the morning to go to work. Can't let that boy cost us a night's sleep. Let's all go to bed," Arthur ordered.

Larry waited patiently until everyone was sound asleep, all snoring contentedly. He noticed it took his mother longer to go to sleep than the others. Being very quiet he crawled out from under the bed, gathered up a sweat shirt, jacket, and tennis shoes, and let himself out the back door. He quickly went behind a large bush by the steps and relieved himself. It had been a long day in more ways than one! Sitting on the back steps he quickly took off his Sunday shoes, replacing them with his tennis shoes. Then he put on the sweatshirt and jacket over his shirt. He took off his tie, folded it neatly and left it with his shoes sitting on the steps.

Spot was watching him intently, head tilted to one side. Larry knelt down, gave him a hug, and whispered in his ear, "Take care of Ernest, old friend. I gotta go!" Spot gave him a puzzled look and whined softly, watching Larry quietly let himself out the gate to go quickly into the night.

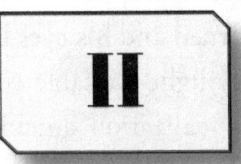

II

Larry had heard the train whistles many times and had been to the railroad tracks a few times with his friends. They had speculated where the trains went and, as boys will do, fantasized about jumping on one of the cars and riding it to exotic adventures in some distant place. The train whistles always reminded him of when he was very young and his family lived in the country close to some railroad tracks. As trains would go by during the night the lonely sounding whistles would sometimes wake him, but instead of frightening him the whistles gave him a feeling of comfort and he would drift back into a sound sleep.

With almost a full moon to light his way on this crisp October night, he was soon at the tracks. He found himself on a low bank about four feet high, paralleling the tracks, and could hear a train coming. A plan quickly formed in his mind.

"This is perfect!" he said out loud, as his heart began to pound and adrenaline began to flow. "Bet I'll be in Memphis or Nashville by morning!" As the train went slowly rumbling by he started running along the bank, trying to match its speed. He had the naive confidence of youth he could do this! Just as he was running out of bank, an empty freight car, with its door open, went noisily creaking by, and he desperately dove for it head first, landing just inside the door, hard!

Laying on the floor of the boxcar, breath knocked out of him, gasping for air, he slowly rolled over on to his back. Looking up and out the open door at the sky, he could see the moon shining through limbs of trees lining the tracks. It appeared to be racing along with him.

His breath slowly returned and his eyes began to adjust to the light inside the boxcar, the only light available coming from the moon. As he lay there recovering, a realization quickly became more clear and very real. This was not a game he was playing with some of his buddies that would soon end, and then he'd return to the safety of his home. He had started on a path to some place he'd never been, and there was no turning back! Returning to his home and the feeling of safety and comfort from familiar surroundings was out of the question and never even crossed his mind. This was a new kind of experience, and with it came a new kind of fear, but he felt no regret for what he was doing.

He crawled to the front of the boxcar trying to get away from the chilly breeze coming through the open door. *"Wish I'd brought my big coat and a blanket,"* he thought to himself. The loud noise level inside the car and jerking from side to side was something he hadn't expected. As the train picked up speed the ride smoothed out just a bit, and soon the events of the day began to catch up with him. The clicking sound of the rails, combined with exhaustion, took over, and he rolled into a fetal position as he fell into a restless sleep.

III

The sudden jerk of the train stopping awoke Larry with a start! Sitting straight up it took a few seconds to realize where he was, and then memory of events of the day came rushing back. He remembered he was in a boxcar on a train. As he cautiously crawled to the open door and looked out, he could still see the moon shining in the dark sky. The moonlight allowed him to see trees and bushes alongside the train tracks, but his sight was blocked beyond that. In the distance a train whistle was blowing; it seemed to be getting closer and louder, and he quickly retreated back to his corner.

Suddenly, on the side he couldn't see, the other train went roaring by, going in the opposite direction of his train, the noise almost deafening, with vibrations causing his boxcar to shudder. It took a long time to pass and he guessed there were at least a hundred boxcars. He realized they were on a siding so they could pass another train on the single track railroad.

It ended as suddenly as it had begun, the sound of the other train rapidly retreating into nothingness. The sound of his train starting to move roared back toward him, like dominoes falling in a line.

Seemingly out of nowhere a large duffel bag landed in the middle of the boxcar, followed immediately by a man smoothly landing on his feet just inside the open door. "Dang, that was close. Almost didn't make it!"

the man said to no one in particular. Framed in the open door, Larry could see he was a small man, smaller than his Dad, wearing a knit skull cap and a Navy pea coat. *"Bet he's warmer than I am,"* Larry thought. The man picked up his bag and moved to the front corner of the car opposite Larry, unaware there was someone else in the car. He sat next to his bag, took a pack of cigarettes from his shirt pocket, bumped one out and put it in his mouth and struck a match to light it. After lighting it he went to shake out his match, and spotted Larry.

Holding the match high as he could, squinting into the dark corner, he said, "Well, well, well! What have we here? Where'd you come from, Kid? Ain't you a little young to be ridin' the rails? You a runaway, Kid?" The match burned his fingers and he slung it toward the open door. "What happened? Yore old man git drunk and start beatin' you agin'? Yeah, been there, done that. That's what happened to me too. That's why I rode these rails the first time." Then thoughtfully, half to himself, " Didn't have much choice really. After I laid him out with my baseball bat I had to leave! Never went back there neither." He took a deep drag off his cigarette and settled back against his duffel bag, looking out the open door, seeming to be reliving the past event in his mind. Snapping back to the present he asked, "Is that what happened to you, Kid?"

Larry was nervous. Having company was something he hadn't thought about and one more thing his frayed emotions didn't need right now. Instinctively he didn't trust or like his new boxcar mate. He wondered which one of his many questions the man wanted him to answer first. Voice cracking, he said, "No, I'm just going to Nashville to visit my Uncle. He's in the music business and I'm going to visit him."

The man got a sarcastic tone to his voice. "Nashville, huh? Rich Uncle, huh? Yeah, I'll bet! Well lookie here, Kid, you done hopped the wrong freight. This here train is headed to Atlanta, an' we're almost to the Georgie line." He stared into the distance and took another long drag off his cigarette. "You know what I think Kid? I think you hopped the first freight that come along. I just bet you was in sech a hurry to get away you didn't much care which way you went!"

"How did he know?" Larry thought.

They were moving along at a pretty good pace now. Being quiet for a couple of minutes, the man finished his cigarette and flicked it out the open door. He seemed to be in deep thought.

Starting to talk again, he said, "My names Buford, Kid, Buford Sledge. What's yores? How old are you?"

"My names Larry Thedford and I'm sixteen."

"Sixteen, huh? Yeah, I'll bet. Listen Kid, if yore gonna ride these rails, you need a buddy, and you don't need to lie to yore buddy! We gotta look out for each other, see?

"Look kid, things ain't been too good for me lately. You got any money? We need to share money too."

Now Larry had one dollar in his pocket he had intended to put in the collection plate at church, and forty-seven cents he'd saved from his lunch money at school, but he sure didn't feel like sharing with Buford. "No, I left so quick I didn't have time to pick up any money," he said.

Buford rolled his eyes again. "Larry, now look here Kid, remember what I said about not lyin' to yore buddy? You seem to have a habit of lyin'. Is that why yore ol' man was beatin' you?" With a quick and smooth motion he pulled something from his hip pocket. "Have you seen one of these?" Larry heard a click and saw the glint of moonlight on steel and his heart jumped into his throat. "It's a switchblade knife, Kid, and it's sharp as a razor! You know, if somebody was to cut yore throat and throw you off this train they'd probably never find yore body, and if they did they wouldn't ever know what happened to you. Come here, Kid, let's have a look at what's in yore pocket!" He made a threatening move toward Larry.

All Larry could think was he was gonna get his throat cut and his body would never be found. Fear, combined with the state his emotions were in, was too much. His adrenalin and survival instinct kicked in and he panicked. In a flash he was headed for the door, and left the boxcar the same way he came in, head first, into the darkness.

"Dang fool Kid," Buford said, moving to the door. "I was jest tryin' to skeer him a little bit! Didn't mean to make him kill hisself.' And then thoughtfully, "Hope he didn't get away with no money!" He was standing in the open doorway, squinting into the darkness, when the boxcar made one of its sideways jerks as they started over a trestle. Losing his balance, Buford went tumbling out, clawing at the air, desperately trying to reach back in, and gave a short scream just before his head hit the steel framework of the trestle with the sickening sound of "thwack"! His limp body went tumbling through the framework, down, down into the cold dark water of the Tallapoosa River. The empty boxcar with the duffel bag went rumbling on toward Atlanta.

IV

Diving out of the boxcar into the darkness and the chilled October air, Larry seemed to fall forever before he hit the downslope of the railroad bed. Tumbling wildly, rocks and cinders digging into his skin, vines and bushes and briars tearing at his clothes, he slammed into something big.

* * *

His first awareness was of being carried; then light, a soft light, as consciousness began to return ever so slowly. Then he was lying on something soft, could feel warmth and hear a crackling sound. Straining to focus his eyes, he could tell he was lying in front of a large stone fireplace with a blazing fire going. "You're safe now, Child. You gonna be just fine," a soft mellow feminine voice said.

"Am I dead? Is this Heaven?" he asked, slowly turning his head toward the light and the warmth of the fire. Painful zigzag patterns of light went flashing through his eyes. Trying to locate the source of the voice, a fuzzy face slowly came into focus, and he found himself looking into the most beautiful warm brown eyes he'd ever seen.

The eyes were in the face of a beautiful woman, dark complexion, with long straight black hair. She was about the same height as his mother, but slimmer, and stood very straight. For some reason, even in

15

his confused and semi-conscious state, she made him think of Pocahontas and the way he had always imagined the Indian princess looked.

"No Child, you're here with us, Luke and me," she said as she softly chuckled. "You just take it easy and rest; don't try to move much just yet. You had a right nasty fall, and you got a big gash on the side of your head. Spirit was looking out for you or you'd be in Heaven right now!" she said.

"Is he back with us, Angel?" Larry heard a deep male voice ask. He looked past the lady and saw a big man with a wide grin. He too had dark skin, long straight black hair pulled back into a ponytail, and shoulders that seemed to stretch out forever. His face was clean-shaven, with high cheekbones, and in his confused state Larry thought, *"This must be Pocahontas's husband."*. "Welcome back Son," he said. "You had us a little worried there for a while. You been asleep for two days an' we was wondering when you was gonna wake up."

Suddenly Larry had a flashback! He tried to sit up, but the pain in his head pushed him back down, flashes of white light obscuring his vision. "Is Buford here? Is he coming? He's got a knife….." and his voice trailed off.

Immediately the lady touched his cheek with the palm of her hand, and then gently stroked his hair. "No Child, ain't nobody here but us three and Spirit. You're safe. Luke and me ain't gonna let nobody bring harm to you!" she said, as she continued to gently stroke his hair, and rub the back of his hand. "Now you drink this willow bark tea I fixed for you to take away some of your pain." When she mentioned tea, Larry realized how thirsty he was. The beautiful lady supported his head, and he sipped the tea until it was all gone. She made another cup and he drank that too.

Looking up into those beautiful brown, compassionate eyes, feeling the warmth of the fire, and the softness of his bed, he began to feel safe and comforted. Sinking further back onto the pillow he surrendered to the black wave that swept over him.

For the next few days Larry slipped in and out of consciousness. The fourth day he felt better and sat up in a chair, ate some warm chicken soup and cornbread, and drank some herb tea the lady brewed for him. After five days he could limp around outside. Luke showed him where the privy was, told Larry he was tired of carrying his slop jar! Larry's face turned red, and he tensed up as he stole a glance at Luke, and then relaxed when he saw the mischievous grin.

About a week had gone by, and one evening after they'd finished supper, Luke came bringing in a large rectangular galvanized washtub, sat it in the small kitchen floor, and filled it half full of warm water, heated on the cast iron wood cook stove. "Ok Son, time to take a bath. The air's gettin' a little strong around your bed, and Angel will change your bed clothes while you're bathin' yourself. We got some clean clothes for you to put on when you're finished."

"Clean clothes. Where did you get those?" Larry asked.

"Sometimes I walk into town to pick up a few things we need, so I stopped by the second-hand store, just a block off the town square," Luke said. "They had some clothes about yore size, well maybe just a little big, but you'll grow into 'em. Angel has done washed 'em just to make sure they're real clean! Take yore time gittin' yore bath. You still got some sore spots, an' we ain't in no hurry."

Larry was bashful like most thirteen-year-old boys, but there was a sheet hung to give him some privacy. The beautiful lady Luke called Angel had been giving him sponge baths while he was bedridden and putting ointment on his cuts and skinned places and changing the bandage on his head. She had begun to assume a mother image in his mind and that helped with the bashful issue. It was painful at first, as he slowly worked his way down into the tub, with the occasional sharp intake of air through clenched teeth as his skinned and scabbed over places met the water, but the warm water helped his healing skin relax and it soon began to feel good.

"Child, are you alright?" Angel asked from across the cabin.

"Yes, M'am, I'm fine," he answered, picking up his washrag and soap and getting started.

Feeling much better when he finished his bath, he quickly dried with a clean towel, put on his fresh clothes and went to the fireplace to get warm. Angel and Luke were sitting on the couch, and Luke was sipping his usual evening cup of hot coffee, so Larry sat on the big overstuffed chair.

"Here's your clean socks, Child. They're about the only thing that didn't get tore up in your fall, along with your shoes. One of them was missing when Luke brought you in, but he went back and found it later," Angel said, as she handed the socks to him.

"Thanks, M'am."

Luke said, "It was lying close to that big railroad switch box you hit, and that switch box is what give you that big gash on the side of yore head. It's probably the only thing that kept you from going into the river too, and if that'd happened you'd still be at the bottom of the Tallapoosa!" Luke said as he leaned back and took a sip of coffee.

"How'd you come to find me?" Larry asked.

"Lucifer told me."

"Lucifer?"

"Yeah, my pet crow. I call him Lucifer 'cause of his devilish ways," Luke chuckled. "He hangs around outside the cabin waitin' for a handout and will eat just about anything, so we give him some scraps, and he acts like they're real treasures. That morning he was actin' all excited, makin' lots of noise, and kept flying off toward the railroad track, so out of curiosity I followed him. He led me straight to you! You might say ol' Lucifer saved yore life."

All Larry could say was a long drawn out, "Wow!"

"You know Son, you been here a little over a week now, and I think it's time we got better acquainted. I'll start it off. You already know my name is Luke. This here beautiful lady is Evangelina, but I just call her Angel 'cause that's what she is to me."

She patted the back of Luke's hand and gave him that adoring look Larry had seen many times during the past week. "Now it's yore turn. What's yore name, Son?"

"Larry Thedford and I'm thirteen."

"Yep, that's about the age I figured, but I wouldn't a' been a bit surprised if you'd said fourteen or fifteen. You're a right good size for your age. Must a' been eatin' lots of good butterbeans and turnip greens!" Luke chuckled. He continued, "Larry. Now that's a good name, and you seem to be a fine young man. We noticed you're real polite, and even though they was tore up pretty good, you had on some right nice clothes when you got here, so we figured you come from a purdy good family." He noticed Larry's eyes began to tear up at the mention of family, so he figured he'd said enough about that for awhile. "Now you can tell us more when you feel like it. There ain't no hurry, like I said before."

Larry didn't immediately say anything, just stared into the fire and swallowed hard, so Luke went on. "I'm gonna tell you some more about us. We've already talked it over and Angel said it was ok. I'm sure you noticed our dark skin an' you may be wonderin' where we come from. Well, one of my ancestors was a slave, one was a Indian, an' still another was a white man."

"Are you part Cherokee?" Larry asked.

"No, but I get asked that a lot. I'm Choctaw! One of my ancestors was Chief Tuskaloosa!" Luke said proudly. "I was born in a small village between Selma and Mobile, an' I worked on a big cotton farm. World War II come along, an' I joined the Army, along with some other young Choctaw Braves, an' they put us to work in what they called the intelligence service. Seems there was a tradition of 'code talkers' started in World War I by the Choctaw Indians, where we would communicate important military things in our native Choctaw language. The enemy never did break 'the code,' which was just us talkin' in our own Choctaw language." Luke leaned back and let out a big belly laugh. He was obviously enjoying the memory. "After the war I went back to the farm. I'd seen a lot of new things and places, had lots of interestin' experiences, but I was happy to git back home. There just ain't no place like home!" A big grin spread across Luke's face.

Larry, completely captivated by what he was hearing, sat with his eyes and mouth wide open, as though he was hypnotized!

Luke finished his coffee and sat the cup down. "This may be more than you can digest right now, Son, but there's a reason I'm tellin' you all this," Luke said. "Now Angel was born in the same village I was and worked on the same farm. My daddy was killed in the coal mines when I was a baby an' I never knowed him. Angel's mother was never really sure who her Daddy was. She was pretty sure it was a evangelist that was passing through, so they named the baby Evangelina.

"Her ancestry mix is about the same as mine, but her skin turned out a little lighter. I always thought she was the most beautiful woman in the world, but I never thought she'd be interested in me."

Angel spoke up. "I tried and tried to get him to notice me but he never seemed to take the hint." She smiled and sighed flirtatiously.

Luke went on. "Then the farm overseer took a shine to her an', to make a long story short, took her for his wife. He turned out to be a mean sort and would beat her when he took a notion, usually when he was drinkin' some of that rot gut whiskey they made down in the woods on the farm.

"One day out in the barn she was gatherin' eggs, and he come up behind her an' surprised her. It made her jump, and she dropped the eggs an' broke most of 'em. Now that made him mad an' he drew back with the rope he was carryin' to hit her.

"What he didn't know was I was standin' right behind him an' automatically just reached out, grabbed the rope an' yanked it!" Luke went through the motions of what he was saying, seeming to relive the incident in his mind. He was staring straight ahead. "He lost his balance and fell back on to a scythe that was leanin' against the wall.

The blade went in his back right between his shoulder blades and come out just above his left nipple. He never knowed what hit him! It all just happened so quick." Luke took a deep breath and blew it out and kind of deflated..

"Well, it was a accident, but we knowed we'd be blamed for killin' him, him bein' the overseer an' all, so we left right then. We made our way to the railroad and ended up ridin' the same train probably you come on. When it stopped at the sidin', about a mile down the railroad, we got off.

"We got real lucky an' found this cabin an' spent the rest of the night sleepin' inside here. Early the next morning, the owner, Mr. John Sorenson, was taking a walk to go down by the river and found us sleepin'. I guess we was oversleepin' 'cause we was so wore out from all that happened the day before. Anyhow, he turned out to be a real good Christian man; told us we could stay here if we'd fix up the cabin a little bit. He could probably tell by the look on our faces we was just about at the end of our rope and needed a helping hand. He even invited us up to his house for breakfast!

"Well, carpentry is one of my favorite things to do, so I took him up on his offer, and it worked out real good. He bought the stuff I needed, and I fixed up the cabin. He never asked us anything about how we got here. Guess he figured he didn't need to know, or maybe he knew we'd just tell him a good story anyway.

"He pays me for carpentry work on his house from time to time and he buys some of the fish I catch out of the river. That man loves fried catfish! Well, at first we ate a lot of fish out of the river too. Mr. Sorenson made sure we had some veggies to eat, mostly greens and taters 'til our own garden got goin', an' gave us a few chickens he said he needed to git rid of anyhow. It didn't take long for our own greens to start growin'. I sell lots of the fish in town, and that gives us enough money to buy a few things we need, mostly flour, salt an' pepper, an' some coffee. We get what clothes we need from the second-hand store in town. Most of our food comes out of the garden an' the woods an' the river, so we don't need much. We've been here a little over a year now. Now that we got the garden goin' real good an' been able to git a few things we need, we got a purdy good life. We're happy as two peas in a pod an' thank Spirit every day for takin' such good care of us! Is that too much information for you, Son?" he asked, grinning.

Mesmerized, Larry slowly shook his head no, eyes and mouth still wide open.

Angel had been quiet while Luke talked, sitting next to Luke and slowly rubbing his forearm, listening intently to what he was saying. "Child, that's a lot to take in all at once. You're the only one besides us that knows this story. We feel you've been directed here by Spirit, just like we are. We feel like you're a special person, even if you don't know it yet, and we can trust you with the whole story. Later, you may need to know even more. Only Spirit knows what's gonna happen in the future.

"We're just so happy Spirit directed you our way and is allowing us to be of help to you. Luke and me decided some time ago we would spend what time we have left on this earth helping whoever Spirit sends our way, just like Mr. Sorenson did us. There are so many troubled souls that just need a helping hand and a safe and warm place to rest!"

She leaned over and took his hands into hers and continued talking. "I know you have things you need to share with us, 'cause along with a damaged body you got a damaged soul! Somebody has betrayed you and it hurt you right down to your core! As long as that hurt stays inside you, it will just get worse, and will fester and grow and do more damage. You got to get it out! You got to learn to trust us enough to let us share the load of your hurt!"

Recollections of whippings, humiliation in front of his friends, many nights when he cried himself to sleep, came rushing to his memory. There were other nights when, after coming home from a revival meeting at church and listening to the evangelist rant and rave, he was too afraid to go to sleep, afraid he would die during the night and go to Hell. He would hold his eyes open as long as he could, fighting sleep, but in the end sleep always won. Sometimes he would have nightmares during those times. He could recall earlier years when there were no whippings, when he looked forward to doing things with his Dad, his hero. Then things began to change.

Larry couldn't put his finger on anything specific, on any one big event, but it seemed to be right after an evangelist, Brother Huffstutler, stayed with them for two weeks while he held a revival at their church. The preacher and his dad spent a lot of time in private conversation. After that his dad stopped doing things with him, never had time to do anything but work. He stopped allowing him and Ernest to go to any socials, or to even go swimming if girls were going to be there; couldn't go to movies, couldn't even mention dancing! Then the whippings started, usually for things that were meaningless to Larry. He felt confused and hurt.

The memories, returning all at once, brought with them a rush of negative emotions. The pressure in his head began to build, and he felt as if it would explode! Larry was overwhelmed with this night; with everything he had learned. All the memories and emotions that had been dredged up were almost too much for a thirteen- year-old boy, already dealing with drastic changes in his life, to handle. But he still loved his dad and was not ready to betray a trust built up during his young life. He put his face in his hands and shook his head no, sobbing, and obviously in a lot of stress.

Angel tenderly put her hand on his shoulder. "It's alright Larry. I understand. There's no hurry. You take your time, as long as you need. We'll be here if you ever need to lean on us, but in the meantime all you're gonna get from us is a lot of love!

"Here, let me get you a cup of willow bark tea to help ease your pain and get a good night's sleep. It's about time we all go to bed," she said, making her way to the kitchen. Soon she returned with the cup of tea and handed it to Larry, then tenderly touched his cheek with the palm of her hand, wiping away his tears that were streaming down his face. "Here Larry, drink this, and get a good nights sleep, and we'll see you in the morning", she lovingly said.

Luke and Angel climbed up to the sleeping loft, and Larry began to sip the tea. It wasn't his favorite drink, but it did help ease the pain in his head.

"*Who's this Spirit?*" Larry wondered. After he finished the tea he made his way to bed by the light of flickering flames from the fireplace, and he lay staring at the ceiling, with everything Luke had told him whirling around in his mind. Soon the tea began to take effect, and the warmth from the crackling fire in the quiet cabin lulled him into a somewhat restless sleep.

V

For the next few weeks, Larry continued to get better. The skinned places and cuts healed, and thanks to the magic of youth, hardly left any scars. The large gash on the side of his head closed, and his headaches became less and less frequent. His left knee was swollen at first, and Angel put a poultice on it, and tied it to his knee with a rag made from one of Luke's old shirts. Luke made him a crutch. It looked like a long T that fit under his arm, and Larry imagined he was Tiny Tim and Luke was Bob Cratchett. Laughing, hobbling around on one leg, he quickly learned to use the crutch and to get around very well. It made Angel and Luke happy and relieved to hear him laugh.

He helped all he could with the garden and chores, and Luke and Angel gave him lots of direction and encouragement. The only vegetables left this time of year were collards and turnip greens, some onions and carrots they dug up, and a few winter squash. There was a hill of potatoes and yams close to the chicken pen, under a mound of sawdust.

The chickens kept them supplied with eggs and occasionally some fried chicken, and every day Luke turned the chickens into the garden so they could scratch up and eat lots of grubs, while depositing much good fertilizer.

Hanging in the smokehouse was a butchered hog and deer; the deer had been skinned, and the skin was in the process of being tanned. Luke explained, "The deer had been clipped by a train. Its hip was broke real bad and I just put it out of its misery. That ol' wild hog was rootin' in our garden at night, so I dug a pit and trapped him. Sure gives us a lot of good bacon and pork chops and a nice pork roast when we want to celebrate, an' we have lots of good from Spirit to celebrate. Spirit does look after his people!"

Larry spent many happy hours with Luke on the river in an old boat Luke found and fixed up. He helped Luke run his trotlines he had set to catch the fish he sold in town. If any fish were left over they would end up on the supper table.

Luke showed Larry where mushrooms grew in the woods, how to tell which to pick and which to leave alone.

Angel would take the food provided to her and work magic with it! In addition to what came out of the garden, there were vegetables she had canned during the summertime, as well as dried apples, canned peaches, and blackberries for pies, honey Luke had gotten from a 'bee tree' he found in the woods that she used for a sweetener, shelled corn out of the garden she ground up into cornmeal to make wonderful cornbread and hushpuppies. Angel knew how to find herbs growing in the woods and by the river, and used them to make the food taste better than anything Larry had ever put in his mouth!

It seemed they always needed more wood for the fireplace and wood-burning stove, and Larry got well acquainted with one end of a crosscut saw as well as an axe. After a few times of trying and frustration, and patient coaching from Luke, he caught on, and learned to pull the saw very well, actually enjoying it. Luke showed him how to split wood with the axe and stack the wood for drying. Soon they had a good supply laid in for the winter.

One of the first things Luke showed him about how to use the axe was about how to trim limbs off a log. "We don't need any accidents with the axe. Lord knows we've had our share of accidents. When yore gonna trim off a limb from a log, make sure the log is between you and the limb you're gonna lop off. That axe is sharp, and it'll cut meat just as good as it'll cut wood!"

With youth working in his favor and the help of Angel's poultices, his knee got well rather quickly, and he soon discarded the crutch.

Larry loved to wake up each morning! By the time he awoke Luke already had a roaring fire in the fireplace, and another fire going in the cook stove for Angel. Soon the cabin was full of the smell of fresh coffee and sourdough biscuits. There would be eggs and bacon frying in the big black skillet and gravy bubbling in the stewer. Breakfast was wonderful!

Larry always looked forward to every meal and no one ever had to tell him to clean his plate. In a few weeks, with all the good food he ate and the good exercise he got from his chores, he began to fill out those clothes from the second-hand store.

Life was good! Larry had learned to trust Angel and Luke. They had gradually and naturally become his surrogate parents without him being aware of it. He had never felt so safe and secure and loved as he did now: yet there were times when he had a vague feeling of dread, and many questions would run through his mind at night just before sleep.

Then the dreams started.

VI

Those times on the river running the trotlines were good and there was a lot of good conversation flowing freely between them. During one of those times Larry asked, "Mr. Luke, I've been meaning to ask you something. Who's this Spirit you're always talking about?"

Luke chuckled. "Why, that's just another word for God, Son," Luke said. "I reckon I use the word Spirit instead of God 'cause of my Choctaw heritage and background. The Elders in our village would speak of The Great Spirit. People use lots of words for God: Father, The Creator, Divine Mind, and lots of others. Feel free to use any word for God that feels good to you. He don't mind! Plus the Bible says God is Spirit and lives inside each of us."

"Spirit feels good to me," Larry said. "I just never heard it used like that before."

"Spirit lives in each of us, Son, just like the Bible says," Luke went on, as he pulled in an empty hook and put fresh bait on it. "That's the Christ Spirit within us. Every human being has a spot of the Christ spirit and dignity in him, although many folks has it hid real good! If we look for the good in everybody we'll find that most people are just naturally good when they have a chance to be." He gently dropped the hook back into the water. "Ok, Son, move us on to the next hook," and Larry began paddling.

"Most of the time, if somebody is being mean or evil, it comes from fear. It's 'cause they're afraid of somethin' or somebody, afraid they're gonna be hurt, and they're just trying to protect themselves. They feel like they have to be meaner than whoever or whatever is threatening them so they'll be safe. Course, it don't usually work that way. That just causes folks to defend themselves like any normal person would, and then it can git to be a vicious cycle. Then somebody has to break the cycle, start things off towards good, and Spirit can help us find the strength to do just that!"

They came to the next marker and Luke pulled up the hook to find a large catfish attached. "We got us another nice 'un!", Luke exclaimed.

"So that's what it means when we're taught to turn the other cheek?" Larry asked.

"Yep, that's about the size of it. It ain't always easy, an' it don't mean we have to let people run over us. We just need to ask for Spirit's guidance when somebody is tryin' to mistreat us or take advantage of us. It's always a good thing to remember to say, 'Spirit, guide me now!' We need to keep a good attitude, too. Our attitude will usually make all the difference in how somethin' turns out," Luke said.

"Is this what you mean, Mr. Luke?" Larry asked. "A boy in our neighborhood gave another boy fifty cents to beat me up. We did have a fight and I won, but neither of us was really mad at the other, and we became best friends for a long time. Is that what you're talking about?"

Luke leaned back and let out a deep belly laugh. "I don't think that's exactly the point, Son, but you had a good attitude and become good friends. At least somethin' good come out of it. Now, if you have a problem to solve, like the one you had when the boy was gonna beat you up, ain't nothin' good gonna happen 'til you take some kind of action to help yourself, like you did. You can pray about it 'til the cows come home, but 'til you take some kind of action to help yourself, ain't nothin' good gonna happen!

"Well Son, I think we got 'bout all the fish we can handle today. Angel will fry up some of these for supper if we git 'em to her in time. Mr. Sorenson just might want some of 'em an' we can smoke the rest. You 'bout ready to head for the house, Son?"

"Yes sir, I sure am," Larry said, and started paddling for the dock. "Mr. Luke, you seem to know so many things. May I ask where you learned all this?"

"Of course, Son," Luke answered. "Most of it comes from Angel. You've probably noticed she has a lot more education than me, an' she talks much better English than I do, an' she shared all this stuff with me. She got a lot of it from a book she found in our village wrote by some man named Emerson.

"I guess because she has such a hold on my heart it made me willin' to listen to her, an' after a while it all come to make good sense. Then I tried some of it for myself an' found out it works! Since I've learned how to talk with Spirit an' trust in what he says to me my life has changed completely, an' even though Angel and me is in the pickle we are in I got peace in my heart, an' I love to share it with people.

"Now all this talkin' has made me hungry. Let's go to the cabin and git ready to eat!"

VII

It was a cool mid-morning on Friday, and Luke and Larry were running trotlines that were set deep, hoping to catch some big catfish. Luke said he knew of some people that were likely to want to have a fish fry soon, and he "could use a little extra money for Christmas, which was just around the corner!" As he was pulling in one of the lines, Luke said, "This must be one of the big 'uns I keep dreamin' about ketchin'. Larry, give me a hand gittin' this 'un in!" Larry moved to the back of the boat and grabbed on to the line with Luke and they began to pull it in. "It's gittin' close, easy now," Luke said. "Good gawd-a-mighty! What's this?"

Larry looked at what had startled Luke and immediately turned loose of the line and sat back into the boat. He instantly recognized the big coat and skull cap, even though he was looking at the back of it. "It's him! It's Buford Sledge!"

Luke reached down and grabbed the coat collar from the back. "Are you shore? How do you know?" Luke asked, still hardly believing what he held in his hand.

"I'd recognize that coat and cap anywhere! I'll never forget it!" Larry said.

"Oh my gawd! How did he get here?" Luke asked. "Never mind! Larry, you paddle us into the dock. I'll hang on to the body."

Larry picked up the paddle and began to move them toward the shore. It was the first time he had seen Luke this upset or had heard him use that kind of language. The body was a drag, but Larry's adrenaline was flowing, and he soon had them in to the dock. Luke had to use all his considerable strength to hoist the waterlogged body on to the dock. The body was bloated, and fish had been nibbling at the face and head. It was hardly recognizable as human. The smell that came from it, combined with the way the face looked, was too much for Larry. He promptly lost his breakfast into the water and spent a few minutes upchucking and gagging. Luke was a little amused, although he didn't feel too good himself.

"What could have happened to him?" Larry asked. "He was fine the last time I saw him. He had that switchblade knife in his hand and was coming for me!"

"Son, we'll probably never know that! Whatever it was had to 'a happened purdy quick after you left the train, 'cause he went into the river! The left side of his head is just about gone, so somehow he musta' got whacked upside the head. Looks like whatever it was, it was quick, an' he was most likely dead when he hit the water," Luke said.

Larry impulsively blurted out, "Can't we just throw him back in the river? He was an evil and mean person!" Larry stood on the edge of the small dock and stared out across the river, intentionally not looking at the body.

"Larry, he was a human being an' a child of God, just like you an' me. He deserves a decent burial, and we're gonna give him one. There's a reason we found him. I don't know what it is just yet, but somehow he was guided to our hook so we'd find him, an' it's up to us to give him a decent burial. We'll give him a Christian burial an' make him a marker as best we can. He's already gone on to his reward anyway, whatever that is."

Not willing to give up on a thought so quickly Larry again impulsively spoke up. "He was an evil man, a sinner! Brother Raeburn said miserable sinners all go to Hell and spend eternity there!"

"Oh he did, did he?" Luke said. "Larry, like I said before, Buford was a child of God, and nothin' can change that fact. It just don't matter what he done while he was alive. Just like the story of the Prodigal Son, his Father was happy to welcome him home, I'm sure. We don't know what happened to make him the way he was, but you can bet your bottom dollar it wadn't good!"

Larry was quiet for a minute and then thoughtfully said, "Well, he did say his Daddy would get drunk and beat him, and I think he fought back one time and beat his Daddy up with a baseball bat, maybe even killed him, and he had to run away."

"There you go!" Luke said, gesturing with his hands, trying to drive his point home to Larry. "Try to put yourself in his shoes. Just think how tough that would be on a kid an' it wouldn't be his fault. He was forced to live a tough life on the run, an' had to get tough hisself in a hurry just to survive. I'll say it again! There's always a reason bad people are bad. What might seem bad to you or me just seemed like common sense to him, just somethin' he had to do so he could live to see the next day! When you think about it, Buford was a purdy remarkable person to have survived as long as he did." Luke put his hands on Larry's shoulders and said in a real thoughtful tone, "A lot of people, probably most, would 'a just took the punishment that was handed out and kinda grinned and bore it, so to speak. As a matter of fact, Larry, you and Buford had a lot in common!"

Larry slowly nodded his head, and thoughtfully said, "Yes, and if he had been lucky enough to have found someone like you and Miss Angel to help him when he needed it, chances are he would have been a completely different person."

"Maybe so Son. We'll never know." Luke took a step toward the body and continued. ""We each have to follow our own path an' play the cards that are dealt to us. Buford did the best he could with what he had, an' really he could 'a done a lot worse."

Luke began gesturing again and said, "Remember what you said about your preacher saying all miserable sinners would spend forever burnin' in Hell? Preachers seem to have a habit of talking mostly about sin an' evil an' we hear a lot more about Hell than we do about Heaven, more about the Devil than about God, more about the fear of dyin' and goin' to Hell than about the joy of livin' an' the peace you have when you follow Jesus' teachings. That stuff drives a lot of people away from church. I know it did me at a early age. A lot of people that stay in church git to be so judgmental they make everybody around 'em miserable, an' really they're unhappy an' live in a little Hell of their own makin'."

Luke faced Larry again. "Larry, all that Hell fire an' damnation stuff didn't come from Jesus' teachings, but it come from early church teachins when they was trying to scare people so they could control 'em. Remember Son, if someone can't scare you they can't control you. Jesus talked about the divinity of man, not about man being a hopeless sinner. Maybe someday you'll learn more about this, but Jesus was convinced of 'the divinity of man' an' talked about it in his teachins." Luke's customary grin spread across his face. "Now, I call these preachers that harp on the negative stuff Brother Badmouths, but that just shows I got some growin' of my own to do too."

Larry was quiet and obviously thinking very hard. He said, "Mr. Luke, I never heard it put like that, but it's beginning to make sense, like everything you say. It just feels real natural. It's a lot to think about."

"Yep, I'm sure it is. I'm sure it's all new to you, a different way of thinkin' an' feelin' than you're used to. I know it was to me for awhile. Talk to Spirit about it and then listen to what He has to say." Luke turned his attention back to the body. "In the meantime, I guess Mr. Sledge has had a purdy good sermon after all, even if it is different from the usual funeral message. I guess it's time for what's left of him to go to his final restin' place. May he rest in peace." And then thoughtfully and under his breath, "I'll just bet he's feeling a lot more peace now than he ever did while walkin' on this Earth!"

They dug his grave close to the woods, in the shade of a large red oak tree. After wrapping the body in an old sheet Angel brought to them, they placed it in the shallow grave and all bowed their heads as Luke said a prayer, then they filled in the grave. Larry wrote Buford's name on a small cross Luke made, and they stuck it in the ground at his head.

Luke said, "I'm sure the 'powers that be' in town would like to know about us finding the body, but me and Angel don't need the publicity. Spirit knows all about it an' that's all that matters! We've done about all we can for Buford so we'll just let Spirit take care of it." They walked slowly toward the cabin, not talking, each with their own thoughts.

That night, and for the next several nights, Larry had trouble getting to sleep. He spent a lot of time thinking about the things Luke had said, and the image of Buford's face kept hanging around when he'd close his eyes to go to sleep.

VIII

Angel announced one morning at breakfast, "My, my, how time gets by! It's only three weeks 'til Christmas and we ain't done any decoratin' yet. Luke, we got to make some wreaths for the windows and one for the door. We got to find a tree and get it decorated. I got cookies to make. There are so many things to do. We just gotta get started today!"

"Ok Angel, ok, we'll get it done! Just relax; we'll get started today. Me an' Larry'll go to the woods an' start lookin' for decoration stuff, an' we'll keep a sharp eye out for a cedar for the Christmas tree. I'll go into town an' pick up some extra flour an' sugar an' whatever else you might need. Just make me a list an' I'll go tomorrow. Larry, you 'bout through eatin'? We'll head out to the woods right away!" Luke said.

Larry took a minute to answer. "Yes sir, I'm almost finished." He seemed to be lost in thought.

They picked up an axe and a large burlap sack before leaving for the woods. The weather was a little cold and mostly cloudy. Larry was wearing his big lined denim jacket, another surprise from Luke, along with a warm corduroy cap with flaps that turned down over his ears; "courtesy of the second-hand store," Luke had said. It kept him warm, and Larry was grateful for it.

It didn't take long to find a holly tree with lots of red berries. Luke cut off several branches and carefully stuffed them into the burlap sack.

Larry spotted some mistletoe in an oak tree and climbed up and picked some and dropped it down to Luke; he put it into the sack with the holly. A cedar tree furnished material for the wreaths.

When the sack was full, Luke carried it and the axe, and Larry carried the cedar branches. They didn't have any luck, however, finding the right cedar for the Christmas tree. "We'll just have to keep on lookin' tomorrow," Luke said. "There's one out there somewhere an' we'll find it, but it's got to be perfect for Angel! Time to head for home."

All the way home Larry was quiet, like his thoughts were someplace else. Luke was used to him talking his ears off, asking all sorts of questions. "Somethin' on your mind Son?" he asked.

After a long hesitation Larry said, "Yes sir, I guess so. Miss Angel talking this morning about Christmas coming reminded me of my family and Christmases we've had. Guess I've been so busy lately with you and Miss Angel I'd kind of put my family out of my mind. Ernest and I always looked forward to Christmas. Mama did too, and I think even my Daddy did."

"I understand Son.," Luke said. They walked on in silence for a few minutes. "I think the time has come for us to have another talk. Tonight after supper we'll have us a nice long talk!"

* * *

That evening they were sitting in front of the fire after supper with Angel still doing the dishes. Luke was sipping his usual cup of steaming coffee. Larry was sitting in the big stuffed chair, staring at the flames dancing back and forth on the logs, making their different colors and whistling sounds. "Beautiful sight, ain't it Son?" Luke asked. "There's just somethin' fascinatin' 'bout a fire that makes everybody want to look at it!"

"Yes sir, I guess so," Larry said after a long wait, continuing to stare into the fire, "but I wasn't really looking at the fire so much as I was thinking about my family. They're really on my mind a lot today."

"I noticed somethin' was," Luke said. "You ain't hardly said a word all day an' that ain't like you. I figured that maybe it being close to Christmas would git you to thinkin' about times past an' your family, which you still ain't told us about. If there ever is a time when families are happy together it's usually Christmas.

"I can still remember when I was a boy. We didn't have much stuff to give each other at Christmas time, as Daddy had already been took from us, but we had lots of love for each other in our hearts! We'd gather roun' the fire a lot like this un', an' Mama would read the Christmas story from the Bible. She would pray an' thank Spirit for all our many blessings, an' then we'd sing Christmas carols an' the good feelings would flow! Them was good times!

"Now tell me about your family, Son. You mentioned Ernest earlier today. Is he your brother?"

"Yes sir, he's a little younger than me but we've always been close," Larry said. "Ernest and I always loved Christmas! We'd get up real early, all excited, and go runnin' in to the tree to see what Santa Claus had left us. It didn't really matter what it was! We'd play with it all day, and just about wear it out! Sometimes we did.

"And then there was my Daddy. He and Mama would watch us open the presents and play with everything, just sitting back with a satisfied look on their faces and holding hands. They'd pass knowing looks back and forth and they'd sit together and talk quietly and smile. They seemed happy.

"I guess Daddy's a good man, and he works every week day at the steel mill. If he's not working at his job he's working on our house. Seems like lately all he has time for is work!" Larry started to get lost in what he was saying, becoming visibly upset, his fist clenched, clouds of anger floating through his eyes. "And lately he's taken to whipping me a lot! At the least little excuse he's ready to pull off his belt or grab the nearest stick he can find and start whipping me! He never has time to spend with Ernest and me but he always has time to give me a whipping!" Once he got started, Larry just kept on going.

"And another thing. He makes us go to church every time they have a service. Every Wednesday night and all the revival services. Sometimes the revival preacher scares me so bad when I get home and go to bed I'm afraid to go to sleep, afraid I'll die during the night and go to Hell! I hate to go to that church!" Larry was obviously becoming quite upset.

"Úh-huh, I see," Luke calmly said. "An' your Mother, what's she like?

Larry's face visibly relaxed. His eyes teared up. "Mama is a sweet, wonderful lady. She always has good food fixed, and keeps our clothes and the house nice and clean. She tries to keep Daddy from whipping me sometimes but he does it anyway. Says it's what the Good Book tells him to do!" Anger again flashed through Larry's eyes.

Luke went to the fireplace, punched up the fire, and added a log to it. He turned around and started talking.

"Yeah. Well, a lot of people with good intentions have that wrong thinking. They think about punishment so much it pushes any thought of compassion or love right out of their mind! They forget Jesus taught love, forgiveness, compassion, the divinity of man, and simple livin'. He didn't teach punishment! He didn't teach judgment! And it's not their fault. They learn the negative things from Brother Badmouth when he's preachin' an' rantin' an' ravin' like somebody possessed with a demon, all in the name o' the Lord! That kind of negative thinkin' seems to run in a lot of churches; as a matter of fact in most of 'em."

Luke went back to his seat. "I'll just bet your Daddy is doin' the best he can, tryin' to raise you right to the best of his understandin' of what Brother Badmouth says. He worries so much about you gettin' caught up with the 'worldly crowd' an' dying and going to Hell he forgets you need to enjoy this life, the one you've been blessed with here and now. Preachers, like the one that scares you so much, have him confused. It's not that he don't love you. He proves he does by goin' to work every day and providin' a good home and livin' for you an' Ernest an' your Mother. He just forgets that you all need his presence an' some fun from time to time as much as you need a place to live an' food to eat. It ain't necessarily his fault. I'll just bet his Daddy is a lot the same way."

"Yeah, he sure is," Larry said. "All Granddaddy talks about is what a bad place this world is and how sinful everybody is."

"I thought so." Luke said. "They mean well but they're just misguided. We can't change 'em, an' we have to live with 'em, so we just have to learn tolerance and patience. We are the only people we can change, Larry, only us. We can ask Spirit to help, an' he will, even if it's just to give us more understandin'."

"I've prayed lots for Daddy to stop whippin' me so much, but it just doesn't seem to change anything. I gave up on that," Larry said.

Usually Luke's manner was blustery and enthusiastic, but he became very thoughtful, different than Larry was accustomed to seeing. Luke gently said, "Maybe it's the way you pray, Son. Try this. When you want to talk with Spirit find a quiet place by yourself, just like the Good Book says in Matthew, Chapter 6, verse 6, '.......Enter into thy closet, and when thou has shut the door, pray to thy Father which is in secret.' And in verse 8, '......for your Father knoweth what things ye have need of before you ask him.'

"Close yore eyes and git still, and let your mind git quiet. Sit in the silence and talk quietly with Spirit. Remember, He knows what's on your heart before you say it. Then the most important part. Sit real still and quiet and listen for His answer.

"Lots of people call this meditation, but I just call it sittin' in the silence."

"How will I know when he answers me?" Larry asked.

"In different ways," Luke said. "Sometimes when you ask a question, an' git real quiet an' still for a while, the answer will just seem to pop nto yore head. Sometimes, when you're waitin you'll get a inspiration or a urge to do somethin'. That's Spirit tryin' to talk to you.

"Remember, the Good Book says that Spirit lives inside each of us. When we git quiet an' still an' sit in the silence Spirit can talk with us. It don't take no special technique, just gittin' still an' quiet an' sittin' in the silence! You git better at knowin' when it's Spirit by practice, just like you git better at anythin'.

"Cryin' an' beggin' won't help when you pray. We're his children and don't have to beg. He don't want his children to beg!"

Larry was looking at him wide-eyed, a look of wonder and fresh comprehension on his face. "Wow, Mr. Luke, that's a whole different way of praying than what I'm used to. That's like having a quiet talk with a friend."

"Yep, now you're gittin' the idea!" Luke said, a big grin spreading across his face, returning more to his usual way of talking. "Spirit loves us and wants to walk with us and share love. He don't judge us real harsh. As a matter of fact He don't judge us at all, an' He don't punish us, no matter what Brother Badmouth says. The God of the ancient Israelites, the God Brother Badmouth is talking about, was sometimes a harsh and cruel God, a vengeful God that would wipe out entire cities and everyone in them. Jesus come along and changed all that. The God Jesus talked about was a God of tenderness, forgiveness, and compassion. An' there ain't no lake of fire called Hell for you to go to after you die! Just put that thought out of your mind. When you was layin' in your bed afraid to go to sleep, you was in Hell, so to speak! Hell an' Heaven is right here in this world, dependin' on your state of mind."

"Wow!" Larry said again. "That's a whole lot different than they teach at that church I've been going to!"

"Yeah, I know," Luke said. "The original Christians knew all this stuff, but somewhere along the way it got all bent out of shape. Larry, you was born knowin' all this. As you git older, an' you spend more an' more time communin' with Spirit, it'll be revealed to you a little bit at a time. You'll continue to grow in knowledge just like the Good Book tells you to do.

"You don't need some Badmouth preacher scarin' you and leadin' you in the wrong direction! Your relationship with Spirit should not be based on fear. You'll most likely meet people who will cross your path you can study and grow with."

Angel came over with a cup of herb tea for Larry. "Well, have you two been having a good talk?"

"Yes Ma'am, we have," Larry said. "My head is spinning from everything Mr. Luke has told me!"

"Well, let me add one more thing," Luke said. "It took a lot of courage for you to git this far, Larry, an' Spirit was lookin' out for you, or you'd a been dead a long time before ol' Lucifer found you beside the railroad tracks and led me to you, so I guess you ain't finished with what you come into this world to do.

"Now I know you got a big decision to make. Me and Angel love you an' you can stay with us from now on if you want to, but you got a family you love, an' they love an' miss you too, I'm sure.

"Tell you what. You take a week to talk it over with Spirit, ask for his guidance an' then listen to it. Then we'll continue this talk. Now you know Angel and me is always here an' ready to talk with you and help you all we can, anytime. All you have to do is ask."

"Yes sir, I know," Larry said.

As she stood up Angel said, "I think it's time we all go to bed and get a good night's sleep. You two got a tree to find tomorrow!"

"Well, I'll go along with that!" Luke said with a grin, standing up to follow her to the sleeping loft. "Good night Son. Sleep good."

"Good night Sir. Good night Miss Angel." Larry finished his tea and set the cup down, deciding to try Luke's way to pray. He got still and quiet and closed his eyes, then began silently asking Spirit for guidance. Immediately his thoughts went to his family, and soon tears began to flow down his cheeks.

IX

The next morning, bright and early, Luke and Larry set off into the woods to find a Christmas tree. Skies were clear and the air was cold. Little vapor clouds formed from their breath, and the ground covering crunched as they walked from the frost that had formed during the night. They had dressed for the cold, wearing caps, coats and gloves, and only carried an axe this trip. That's all they'd need to cut down a small cedar tree.

"Did you sleep good last night?" Luke asked.

"Yes sir, I did, but I dreamed a lot. I've been dreaming a lot lately about my family. They were talking to me, saying they wished I'd come home," Larry said. "Ernest was talking to me a lot about Spot, my dog, saying how he just moped around since I left and wouldn't eat much. What do you think of that, Mr. Luke? It's like they were in the cabin talking to me."

"Uh-huh!" said Luke. "I'll have to do some studying on that!"

"And I tried talking to Spirit like you said, and it was good. Only problem was, I fell asleep in the chair," Larry said, grinning.

"Haha!" Luke let out a laugh from deep inside. "That'll happen sometimes, Son, 'specially in the beginnin', but you'll learn to stay awake with a little practice. Sounds to me like you got off to a good start."

They continued walking in silence for a few minutes. "Hey, look over there!" Luke said, pointing off to their left. "Do you see what I see? Does that look like a perfect Christmas tree to you or what? I believe Angel will just love that 'un."

The cedar was about five feet high and had a perfect cone shape. Looking at it up close, they found an abandoned bird nest in the branches. "Angel will want to leave that nest, let it be part of the decoration," Luke said.

"Yep, I believe it's the one we've been looking for, Mr. Luke. That didn't take very long."

Luke said, "I still got plenty of time to go into town to get the stuff for Angel that she needs to fix up for Christmas!" He brought the tree down with a well placed one- handed chop.

That evening the cabin was a place of happy chaos. Angel was busy baking cookies, while Luke found an old paint bucket, placed the tree in it, and filled it with stones and water. Angel also showed Larry how to make colored chains out of red, blue, and gold paper.

When the cookies were baking and the tree was decorated, Angel and Luke started making wreaths with the extra cedar branches. Larry was observing and handing them cedar branches and holly pieces with red berries that Angel tied with pieces of red ribbon, while Luke kept trying to hold a piece of mistletoe over Angel's head. She pretended to be annoyed, but Larry noticed she had a mischievous grin and was acting coy!

Larry got to lick the cookie dough bowl all by himself! It was a happy time.

Later that evening, a little later than usual, they were drinking some hot chocolate Angel made from the Hershey's Cocoa Luke brought from his trip into town. They ate some fresh cookies Angel let them sample from the kitchen, (".....but only two each!" she had said.) The cabin was full of good smells from cookies baking and fresh scents from evergreen boughs in the wreaths Angel and Luke had put together. Each window was decorated with a wreath, with an extra one they'd made hanging over the fireplace mantle.

Pausing and looking around, Angel said, "Luke and Larry, this is the most beautiful the cabin has looked since we've been here! This is such a happy time. We're sharing so much love, and the cabin is full of loving energy. Spirit has really blessed us. This is what Christmas should always be about, sharing love with family and friends, the way Jesus shared his love with all the world. I don't ever want to leave this place or forget this time together."

"Amen to that, Angel," Luke said, reaching over to take her hand, and firmly but gently press it to his lips. Larry just nodded his head slowly in agreement, almost overcome with the beauty and emotion of the moment.

Later that night, after communing with Spirit and going to bed, Larry's mind drifted back to times when he and Ernest would help their Mother decorate the tree. Everyone would bring in the presents they had secretly wrapped and hidden away and place them under the tree until the floor was covered. They would sneak some cookies and cold milk from the kitchen. Those were happy times too! Memories of them brought an ache to Larry's chest.

Drifting off to sleep, he again had the same dream. It was as if Ernest and his Mom and Dad were in the cabin talking with him, saying how much they missed him, asking him to come home. His sleep was restless and fitful.

For the next few days, Larry spent much time alone communing with Spirit several times a day. He tried to help with the chores, but his mind was elsewhere. Angel and Luke understood what he was going through and gave him all the time alone he needed. They also spent time with Spirit asking that he give Larry guidance.

This was a big decision for a thirteen-year-old boy to make. On one hand he had never been happier than he was right now, here with Angel and Luke, living a life he considered to be ideal, a new adventure every day, full of learning, feeling loved and secure.

On the other hand he had a family that missed him, a family he loved and missed, not to mention his dog Spot.

Then there was his Dad. The memory of the love for his Dad was strong, but now he was afraid of him. The memory of the pain and humiliation of the whippings was still fresh. Just the thought of it made him angry! The last words he had heard from his Dad were threats, promising him a good whipping when he caught him.

Each night, after he fell asleep, he had the same dream, dreaming his family was in the cabin with him imploring him to just come home! After the fifth day he again knew what he was going to do.

"Mr. Luke, may we have a talk?" he asked after supper.

"Why sure Son. Let's go to the fire and get out of Angel's way while she cleans up the kitchen," Luke said. They took their usual seats by the fireplace.

Larry had a very serious look on his face. He leaned forward and held both hands in front of him, gesturing as he talked. "Mr. Luke, I've done a lot of communing with Spirit, a lot of thinking, and I've made my decision. I love it here with you and Miss Angel. I love the way we live, the talks we have, the good feelings we all share. I've learned so much from you I never would have learned any other place. I think the most important thing I've learned is how to pray, to commune with Spirit, and I'll do that for the rest of my life. I've never felt so happy and loved as I do now."

He stood up and turned to face Luke, still gesturing with his hands as he talked. "I love you and Miss Angel. I never want to leave you and Miss Angel, (his eyes filled with tears and his voice began to choke,)…. but I have to. I have to go home. I don't know what Daddy will do to me when I get home, but I'll just have to trust Spirit to look out for me."

For the first time since he'd been there, Larry thought he saw tears beginning to fill Luke's eyes. Luke cleared his throat and said, "Larry, me an' Angel love you too, an' we don't want you to leave, but we know you have to go. You made the decision we both knowed you'd make. We already knowed you are a wise and courageous young man, an' this just shows us even more how much integrity you have. We couldn't be more proud of you. You listened to Spirit an' figured out what you need to do, an' now you're doin' it. You shore gonna make some people real happy for Christmas!" He reached into his shirt pocket and pulled out a small envelope and handed it to Larry. "I kinda figured what you'd decide to do, so I went ahead and got this ticket for you. Just think of it as your Christmas present from Angel and me. Tomorrow morning we'll all walk into town where you can ketch the bus an' go home." Once again, Larry was speechless and awed by the wisdom of this man.

Next morning, after the usual wonderful breakfast, all three of them walked to town. The morning was crisp and clear, and Larry was wearing the coat and cap from the second-hand store. It was a quiet walk. No one said a word. When they were a block away from the MissAla bus station, Luke and Angel stopped.

"This is as far as we're going Son. You'll have to walk that last little bit by yourself. Think you can handle that?" Luke asked.

"Yes sir, I'm sure I can."

Angel handed Larry a small package. "Here's some of the Christmas cookies for a snack. It won't take the bus long to get you home. When you're eating them remember how much we love you, and remember we'll never forget you. It's been such a blessing having you with us!"

Larry grabbed on to her, encircling her with his arms, burying his face into her neck. "I'll never forget you and Mr. Luke either, Miss Angel," he sobbed, tears flowing from his eyes. He knew he was going to miss her warmth, her gentleness, and the spirit of love she always seemed to have.

Angel tenderly took his face into her hands, and turned it so he was looking directly into her soft, brown eyes. She began wiping away his tears with a small handkerchief and said, "There will be times,

Larry, when you will be confused and not know which way to turn. Try to remember to look inside yourself, for deep down in your being you already know the truth. You already know what decision to make, which way to go. Remember this: have patience. Everything happens in its own time, in its own perfect order."

Luke put his big hand on Larry's shoulder. "If you ever need us, Son, just tell Spirit, an' then look aroun'. We'll be there. Better go now or you'll miss your bus."

Larry regretfully pulled away from Angel, gave Luke a quick hug, and hurriedly walked the last block to the bus station. When he got to the station door, he turned to wave one last time, but they were gone, nowhere to be seen. He went through the door and up to the ticket window. "Can I help you?" the ticket agent asked him.

"I'm going to Iron City and I already have my ticket," Larry said, handing the envelope to him.

"Okay, just keep the ticket and give it to the driver when you get on board," he said, as he handed the ticket back to Larry. Peering closely at Larry, he asked, "Do I know you Kid? Don't remember seeing you before."

"I'm not from around here, but I've been staying with Mr. Luke and Miss Angel out at the cabin by the river on the Sorenson place," Larry said.

The agent glanced off to his right and said, "What did you say their names were, Kid?"

"Mr. Luke and Miss Angel," Larry repeated.

"Hmmm. Ok, better get out to your bus. It's ready to leave," the agent said. He watched Larry go out to board his bus, reached for the wanted poster hanging to his right, by the ticket window, and with a sly grin on his lips reached for the telephone.

Larry gave his ticket to the impatient bus driver and found a seat about half way back on the almost empty bus. Just as he got seated the bus started backing out of the boarding lane. He took the cookies out of his pocket and began munching on one.

Scouring the sidewalks of Riverton with his eyes as they were leaving, he hoped to get one last goodbye wave but never did see them.

Heaviness was settling in his chest, a very sad feeling, and for the first time in several weeks he wasn't feeling well and then his head began to throb. He was glad the ride to Iron City was less than two hours.

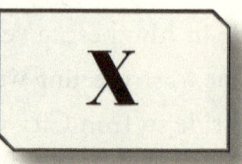

X

Luke and Angel turned and quickly started walking home when Larry was about halfway to the bus station. They were clutching each other's hand, and didn't say a word all the way home. Normally they would have walked to the station with Larry and said their goodbyes there, but what they had not told Larry was when Luke went to the bus station the day before to buy the ticket he had seen the wanted poster hanging by the ticket window. There were no pictures on it, just a description and their names.

They didn't know if there would be a problem, but because they now knew about the wanted poster they were anxious about their situation and fearful about going into town. They realized they would stand out as a couple and people would notice them, even though they were used to seeing Luke when he made his shopping trips into town or would go into town to sell the fish he caught. They were anxious and cautious, listening for any strange sound, and spent a lot of time communing with Spirit and asking for guidance. They didn't sleep very well that night, finally getting to sleep just before dawn.

The day after Larry left, just after dark, headlights suddenly pierced the darkness on the dirt road leading to the cabin. Luke and Angel were immediately aware of it, and they embraced as they looked deep into each other's eyes.

Two cars came roaring up and slid to a stop in front of the cabin; men with rifles and shotguns poured out of all the doors. One of them was the ticket agent from the bus station. They surrounded the cabin.

A loud voice boomed out, "You inside, Luke and Evangelina, this is Sheriff Goolsby from Dallas County. Come out with your hands in the air!" No response. "This is your last chance! Come out with your hands in the air, or we'll come in and get you!" Still no response. "Okay boys, get ready," the Sheriff said. All the men raised their weapons.

Then one of the men hollered out, "Hey Sheriff, the river! There's a boat leavin'! They're trying to git away!" All the men ran to the riverbank. There in the middle of the river, barely visible in the moonlight, was a boat floating away, with a tarp covering something in the bottom of the boat. "Okay boys, we gotta stop em! Let 'em have it!" Twelve rifles and shotguns began to fire continuously. Water around the little boat churned from the bullets and shot hitting it, and pieces of wood from the small boat went flying into the air! Slowly the little boat began to sink and soon disappeared into the dark waters of the Tallapoosa.

The men stood on the bank, silent, staring at the surface of the water where the boat had been. Finally the Sheriff spoke. "Well, I guess we can close this case. They didn't have a chance to get out of that! It's just as well. Saves the state a lot of money trying 'em for murder an' sendin' 'em to the chair. We can go home, back to Selma, an' tomorrow I'll file a report that these two fugitives were killed trying to escape.

"I 'preciate you boys volunteering to be on this posse. Got a couple of bottles of the good stuff we picked up when we raided a still last month, an' we'll taste it on the way home. Let's load up an' go!" The men hurriedly jumped into the two cars, anxious for a taste of "the good stuff." They roared off, with tires spinning, throwing dust and gravel into the air.

Meanwhile, back at the river under the small dock Luke had built, Luke and Angel were holding tight to each other, hardly daring to breathe. "Thank you Spirit!" Angel whispered.

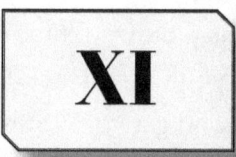

XI

The ride to Iron City was not a lot of fun. Someone in the back of the bus was smoking a cigarette and fouling the air. Larry had forgotten how bad they smelled, and it aggravated his headache and nauseous feeling. The bus route was on a narrow winding road, and the bus driver seemed to be in a hurry, going through turns as fast as he could, throwing passengers from side to side.

Larry tried closing his eyes to ease the pain in his head and the nauseous feeling in his stomach, and it did seem to help. Mercifully he dozed a lot, and once when his head bumped the window hard as they were going through a turn it awakened him, and his head hurt even more.

He was half asleep when they pulled into the station. The sound of air pressure releasing and the driver calling out "Iron City" woke him. Larry was glad to get off the bus, hoping to get a breath of fresh air, but the smell of diesel exhaust wasn't any better than the air he'd been breathing inside the bus.

Walking the seven blocks to his trolley stop, he remembered he'd need money to ride the trolley. Instinctively he put his hand into his pocket. There was the $1.47 he had when he left home, along with a short note. It said, "Thought you might need this. Remember, Larry, everything you need to know is inside you. And remember too, we will always love you and will be there if you ever need us."

"Thanks Miss Angel! Thank you, Spirit, for Miss Angel and Mr. Luke!" he whispered. His head was hurting more and he began to feel like he wanted to throw up.

The trolley soon arrived, number 22, and he boarded it for the twenty-minute ride to his home. Getting off at his stop, he hesitantly walked the half-block toward his house. A woman and a boy were coming out the front door, as though they were going to run an errand. Spot, hanging out in the front yard, was the first to see him and almost knocked him down trying to lick his face.

"Larry, is that you? Oh, thank God you're alive!" his mother said, as she rushed down the sidewalk to embrace him. "Praise the Lord! Our prayers are answered! Let me look at you. Where did you get these clothes? My how you've grown! You're more than an inch taller and you've put on weight! What's this?" She ran her fingers along the scar on the side of his head, blood slowly beginning to ooze through his hair.

"It's a long story, Mama. I'll tell you later. I have a lot to tell you," Larry said.

The sound of the front door opening caused everyone to get quiet and look that direction. His Dad came out the door and down the porch steps and began deliberately walking toward them, unbuckling his belt as he came. "Well, well, the prodigal son returns. You'll find I keep my promises boy!" he said, a sneer on his lips.

Ellen stepped in front of Larry, facing Arthur, and took a step toward him. "Not this time, Arthur, not this time," she said, a cold resolute tone to her voice.

Everything started to whirl around Larry, flashes of light interrupting his vision, the pain in his head becoming unbearable. He reached out to her and said, "Mama......." as he sank to the ground, a familiar black wave engulfing him.

XII

This time was a little different. Almost immediately Larry found himself floating a few feet above his body, looking down on the scene. He no longer felt the pain in his head. He watched as his Mother sat on the ground cradling his limp body in her arms, crying and praying and rocking him gently. His Dad was looking on in shock and disbelief and confusion. Ernest ran into the house to call an ambulance.

Soon the ambulance arrived and the two attendants placed him on the gurney and loaded him into the back of the ambulance, his Mom getting into the ambulance with him, and quickly left for Eastside Hospital, siren wailing and red light flashing with his dad's blue Ford trying to keep up.

Sometimes Larry would be following along floating above the ambulance and sometimes inside the ambulance on the gurney, one attendant sitting beside him with an anxious look on his face. He heard the attendant say to the driver, "We'd better hurry. This kid don't look too good. He's startin' to bleed from his ear!" His Mom was sitting beside him, eyes tightly closed and silently praying, tears running down her face.

Larry thought of Luke and Angel and found himself in the cabin with them. They were sitting on the sofa in front of the fireplace, a good fire going, holding hands, eyes closed, and had a pensive look on their faces. Larry realized they were 'sitting in the silence' communing with Spirit.

A light appeared above the fireplace mantel, and Larry felt himself being pulled toward it, entering a tunnel with a light at the far end, going faster and faster, speeding past little points of light that looked like twinkling diamonds in the night sky. Getting closer to the light, he slowed down and became aware of a being to his left, a being that glowed with a beautiful light. He intuitively knew the being was there to guide him through whatever he was about to experience.

They approached the source of the light, and everything glowed with the brightest, most beautiful light he had ever seen. It was extremely bright, but the light didn't hurt his eyes at all, and he could look directly at it. The light radiated a feeling of peace, and Larry felt more love than he had ever known. He felt absolutely no fear, just great peace, happiness, and joy. He knew he never wanted to leave this place.

"This must be Heaven," he thought, and though he couldn't see his face, Larry knew his guide smiled.

They seemed to glide along wherever his guide wanted to go. His guide directed him toward a large structure. As they got closer he could smell a wonderful fragrance, much like the wisteria blossoms he had smelled at his grandfather's place in the country, except more fragrant.

They approached the structure, and again Larry instinctively knew this was where he would gather much knowledge, and he eagerly looked forward to it. He was hoping he could ask questions because his head was filled with them.

A blue light began to glow and pulsate from within the structure as they approached. Entering, Larry moved toward a small platform, the source of the blue light, and it grew brighter and expanded to encompass him. His guide had stayed on the outside of the building.

The feeling of peace and love inside him, already higher than he'd ever experienced, increased by a factor of at least ten. The blue light seemed to know all his questions before he asked, and the answers flowed into his mind. He spent a period of time inside the blue light absorbing information, feeling amazed at the things he was taught. When the blue light shrank back and he was no longer encircled, Larry knew the time of instruction was over. He couldn't tell how long he'd been there; perhaps a few minutes, perhaps a few hours; time seemed to have no relevance here.

His guide said to him intuitively, "That's all for now. It's time for you to go back."

"Go back? Back where? You mean back to Earth? But I don't want to go back. I just got here. I want to stay. I love it here!" Larry protested.

His guide moved in front of him, pushed the palms of his hands together, smiled and said, "I know young one, but you haven't completed your mission on Earth. You've absorbed much knowledge very few souls are privileged to know, even though you are still quite young in this incarnation. There are many people who need to share in your new knowledge.

"Spirit recognizes you are capable of doing the things assigned to you. Think of this visit as a short rest, a confirmation of the forces in the universe there to support you, and you may call upon them when you need them. There will be trying times when you want to quit, give up, but those are the times to remember Spirit will always be with you. Never quit, never give up! We will meet again in the future." He began to fade away.

"Wait, wait, don't go away" Larry protested, but quickly found himself in a room filled with people dressed like medical personnel, all surrounding his bed and looking anxiously at his body which he could see from where he was floating close to the ceiling. One man he guessed to be a doctor, with strange looking paddles in his hands, applied one to his body's chest and one to his side, and then called out "Clear!" There was a jolt that lifted his body from the bed. With a 'swoosh' Larry was back in his body.

The pain returned.

XIII

Bright lights above his head increased the pain, causing him to turn his head to the side and close his eyes tightly. Immediately the doctor gave an order, "Turn off the overhead lights!" A nurse quickly flipped a switch on the wall; the bright spot-lights over the bed went out and gave Larry a little relief from the pain. He heard a nurse saying, "Blood pressure coming up, 127 over 93, respiration 85. He's back with us, doctor."

The doctor exhaled through puckered lips. "Welcome back, young man. You had us worried for a while! Just try to relax and take it easy as much as you can, and now we're going to make you feel better." He nodded to a nurse and she injected some liquid into a tube that was attached to a needle inserted into the back of his left hand. Immediately the pain in his head began to subside and he cautiously opened his eyes, but just to a squint.

The doctor continued, "Try to keep your head as still as possible. You've had a nasty blow to the side of your head in the not too distant past, and it caused a hairline fracture to your skull. Looks like it was beginning to heal, but it appears to have gotten bumped again re-injuring it and caused you to pass out. We're going to take good care of you and make sure it doesn't get bumped again."

Feeling very tired, the pain killer taking effect, Larry closed his eyes and drifted off to sleep. For the next several days he spent a lot of time sleeping. Life became a blur of nurses taking care of him; changing the huge bandage on his head, giving him medication, bringing him meals, checking his temp and pulse and other vital signs. He never got used to using a bed pan and was always embarrassed when a nurse had to take care of that.

He learned he was in the emergency room of Eastside Hospital. The doctor came by every day to check on him and write new orders for the nurses. His mom was there every day. His dad came a few times but seemed ill at ease, like he didn't know what to say or how to act. Ernest came with his mom a lot and kept him up to date on what was happening with Spot.

Gradually his headaches lessened. He became more aware of his surroundings and was more restless. His doctor was pleased with his progress, and after four days he was transferred to a private room.

The very first thing he did was to get out of bed and try to go to the bathroom, almost falling to the floor. In a flash his Mom and Ernest were by his side to support him! "You're going to have to take it easy Larry, and be more careful!" his Mom exclaimed. "The doctor said you'd be dizzy for a while. He also said you'd try to do too much too soon and warned we'd have to keep an eye on you, and to make you let us help you! You just have to be more patient, and give yourself more time to heal! You sure don't want to fall and bump your head again."

"Ok Mom, you're right. Maybe I don't feel as good as I thought I did. Wow, did I get dizzy in a hurry!" Ernest carefully helped him into he bathroom. There Larry found bars on the wall he could hang on to for assistance and assured Ernest he would be alright and insisted Ernest give him some privacy!

He soon adjusted to his new routine and learned to ask for and accept help, even though he had always been independent, preferring to do things for himself. Time went slowly by and he steadily made progress.

In the middle of January he had his fourteenth birthday, and the nurses on the floor surprised him with a birthday party; a small cake with some candles, and they sang happy birthday to him. The cute little candy stripper, Bernadette, the one that always caused him to have feelings of expectancy and confusion at the same time, kissed him on the cheek, then flirtatiously said, "Happy birthday, Larry!" He thought he was gonna explode! They all signed a single card and gave it to him. Bernadette had drawn a little heart after her signature.

His family all showed up that evening with presents. They also brought gifts from the kids at his church, mostly small amounts of money, from one to five dollars tucked into birthday cards. All together he had a total of forty-eight dollars!

Feeling better and better, he began to remember what happened while he was unconscious and actually clinically dead at times, so he was told. He remembered being out of his body and watching things happen: the ambulance ride, his visit to Mr. Luke and Miss Angel, the trip through the tunnel to the light, his time in that wonderful place he called Heaven, the time inside the Blue Light, and finally returning to his body in the hospital.

At first he just lay and looked at the ceiling, letting the memories return, trying to process what happened. When the doctor made his rounds the next morning, Larry told the doctor about his out of body experience, and asked him what it was all about. The doctor looked at him intently for a long time and then told him he'd obviously had a dream and hallucinations, and to let him know if it happened again and he'd prescribe medications to help him sleep.

Larry thought to himself, *"I'm sleeping just fine, and I wasn't dreaming. I visited Mr. Luke and Miss Angel, and then went to Heaven!"* He didn't want any more medications to take, so he decided not to say anything else to the doctor about it. He just said, "Yes sir."

He started to tell his favorite nurse about it but then had second thoughts. He was afraid she'd tell the doctor, and the doctor would prescribe more medications.

When his mom and Ernest arrived that afternoon, he tried to tell them. It didn't take long for his mom to get really upset and start crying, saying "No one ever went to Heaven and came back. That's not what we learned in Church, and I'll have Brother Raeburn come by and pray for you. The old Devil must be playing tricks on your mind!"

Ernest just looked at him, not saying a word.

Sure enough, the next evening Brother Raeburn showed up, along with his Sunday school teacher, Sister McDougal, and Sunday school superintendent, Brother Davis. They all stood around his bed with a serious and worried look on their faces. Brother Raeburn put his hand on Larry's shoulder and joined hands with the other two. They all began to pray at once, loud and long, asking God to "…….defeat the old Devil and heal Larry's mind."

Well, that went on for several minutes, and Larry sure was glad the door to his room was closed! He was tempted to tell these good people about Matthew 6.6, and sitting in the silence, but somehow he didn't think they'd get it!

XIV

fter everyone left Larry did spend a long time sitting in the silence communing with Spirit, asking for guidance. As he sat waiting for an answer he soon realized it would be best to exercise as much patience as he could, and he decided to keep his out of body experiences to himself. He remembered what Angel had said about the answers being inside him and decided to find answers to his questions there. Then in a moment of clarity he realized he was receiving the answer to his request from Spirit.

His mind drifted back to just five months ago, back to that moment when he'd had enough, had all the pain and humiliation he was willing to take from his Dad, and blindly followed his instincts. He'd had more than one life-changing adventure since then: from diving into the boxcar, to his encounter with Buford Sledge, and diving back out of the boxcar into the night, to being rescued by Luke, nurtured by Angel, and taught so much by both of them. Then there was his trip to "Heaven" and his waking up in the emergency room. It all seemed to have happened such a long time ago, yet was as clear as if it had happened yesterday.

There was a surreal feeling to the entire experience, but here he was in Eastside hospital recovering from a serious injury to his head. All he had to do was touch the huge bandage on his head and look at his surroundings to know it absolutely was real! His journey through the tunnel and the knowledge he'd absorbed from the blue light was all as real to him as the bandage on his head. His new way of thinking; living in the cabin with Luke and Angel; these things were his reality now.

Then there was the problem of dealing with his dad. He hadn't quite figured that out yet. Something he overheard his dad say to his mom, during one of his few visits, bothered him. He had said, "Brother Huffstutler told me to expect the Devil to try and take over his life as he got older, and that I needed to really clamp down on him to not let him drift into the things the Worldly crowd had to offer, and that's what I was trying to do." She had just looked at him and then rolled her eyes and sighed.

And there was Ernest and his mom, something else he was still working on. Though he loved them dearly he just didn't feel comfortable with them anymore. Somehow he felt like he had outgrown them. His mom was convinced he was being taken over by the Devil in his dreams. Ernest just looked at him suspiciously and hardly ever said anything to him anymore.

One thing Ernest did say on about his second visit was, "Spot won't play with me anymore and just mopes around. I'm tired of feeding him and trying to get him to play. Daddy said he is just a nuisance, and we will soon take him to the dog pound." That really upset Larry and caused him to feel very anxious!

Brother Raeburn and the other people from his church really made him feel uncomfortable! He felt totally foreign to their world.

He just wasn't the same naïve boy he'd been when he left on that fateful moon-lit night back in October. He felt a lifetime older.

As though to interrupt his thoughts, there was a soft knock on his door, and it slowly opened. He glanced up and could hardly believe his eyes! Quietly coming through his door, grinning from ear to ear, was Luke, and right behind him was Angel. "Mr. Luke, Miss Angel, where did you come from? How did you know I was here? Luke, why are you wearing that doctor's coat? This is great! I was just thinking about you."

"Shhh Son, hold it down," Luke said as he quietly closed the door behind them. "We don't want to attract the attention of the nurses this time of night. As for my coat, you'd be surprised where you can go in a hospital if you wear one of these, carry a piece of paper, keep lookin' at it an' walk real fast! People just naturally assume you're a doctor with his nurse an' on the way to see a patient. Ha ha ha!

"We wanted to tell you about the changes in our life and looked up the phone number to your Daddy's house. We called it, an' yore mom said you had a accident an' was in the hospital, even told us what hospital, an' here we are!" Luke said.

"It's so good to see both of you!"

"It's so good to see you too, Larry. Tell me, how are you feeling? Why are you here?" Angel asked, touching the bandage on his head.

"I'm a lot better Miss Angel. It seems I had a hairline skull fracture, I guess from hitting the big switch box when I jumped off the train. The doctor said I'd had some good care, and it was healing just fine until it got bumped; on the bus ride to Iron City, I suppose."

"Oh my! Then you needed to be in the hospital all this time! Spirit has a way of working things out the way they should be," Angel said.

"I guess so," Larry said. "It's so good to see both of you. I have so much to tell you! I actually got to go to Heaven and visit and learn. I wanted to stay, but they sent me back; said I still have things to do. On the way there I went by the cabin. You looked like you were communing with Spirit at the time."

"We have a lot to tell you too, Son," Luke chimed in. "We was paid a visit by a posse from Selma, an' now we're officially dead, gone to the bottom of the river! Thanks to some good advice from Spirit and a dim moonlight night, the only thing that's dead is that ol' rowboat we used to haul in our fish. It's at the bottom of the river. Ha! We've been hanging out here in Iron City with a ol' friend from the village we grew up in, feller called Little Bit; drives a taxi."

"Wow! I want to hear more about that! I hope you can stay awhile," Larry said.

"We can stay a little while, Larry," Angel said. "We want to hear all about your trip to Heaven and what's happened to you since you've been here."

"It's a long story I look forward to telling you, sitting in front of the fireplace at the cabin with one of Mr. Luke's fires going. I've missed those times so much!" Larry said. Then his expression and demeanor turned anxious. "Mr. Luke, Ernest said Daddy is going to take Spot to the pound! What can I do about that?"

Luke and Angel solemnly looked at each other, and then back at Larry. "Son, I'm truly sorry to hear that about Spot! I'll think on it, but did you hear what I just said? We can't never go back to the cabin! We officially died there and are at the bottom of the river. It made big news in Riverton. They've probably quit draggin' the river for us by now an' just assumed we washed on down the river someplace, an' that's just fine with us!" Luke said. "I'm sure they found Buford's grave too, an' they're havin' a good time figurin' out that mystery! Just imagine the stories they can come up with. I don't wish to shed any light on what really happened! They'll be happier with their own imaginins'."

"But what are you going to do?" Larry anxiously asked.

Luke answered, "It's amazin' how Spirit will open new doors when old ones close. I have a ol' buddy I grew up with, Jerry David Randleman. Everybody called him JD. Used to pick cotton with him. He was more serious-minded than I was. Then he went off to a school somewhere in the Midwest, close to Kansas City I think. He's now a preacher in the Cherokee Nation in the Smokies. Seems his little church is in bad need of some repair work. I had called him before you showed up at the cabin, when we was tryin' to figure out what we was gonna do next. We knowed we wouldn't be able to stay at the cabin forever, no matter how much we loved it! So we're goin' up there for a while an' just follow Spirit's guidance the best we know how! Gonna catch the train in two days."

"I want to go with you!" Larry said.

"Larry, that might not be the best idea," Angel said. "We'd love to have you, but you have your family now. What would they do? They'd miss you terribly!"

"I'm not so sure about that!" Larry said. "Daddy hasn't changed a bit! He was taking his belt off to whip me when I passed out and had to go to the hospital. I think he's just waiting for me to get well and come home to pick up where he left off. Ernest will hardly talk to me since I made the mistake of trying to tell them about my trip to Heaven! Mama is convinced the Devil is taking over my mind in my dreams. I'll miss her, but I could let her know I'm ok, and I could call her from time to time. I just don't feel I belong here anymore! I don't want to go back to that old life I had before I left. People from the church came by, and they're convinced I'm being taken over by the Devil too! Talk about feeling out of place. I just can't go back to that life!" He paused as if in deep thought. He looked up at Luke and Angel and said, "If you won't take me with you I'll come by myself and find you."

Luke started grinning. "Now that might not be too good, what with your history of travelin' alone. We'll all have to talk with Spirit about this an' listen to his advice. There's another little issue too of being charged with kidnapping of a minor! Me an' Angel don't need that to deal with! Right now it's time for us to go, an' we have to try an' sneak outa' here without attractin' too much attention."

Angel bent down and gave him a kiss on the cheek. "Larry, talk with Spirit, and we will too. We'll talk to you before we leave." They moved toward the door.

"Ok. Goodnight Miss Angel. Goodnight Mr. Luke."

Luke opened the door cautiously just a bit and carefully looked down the hall, signaled for Angel to follow him and started walking quietly and rapidly toward the stairwell.

Larry got out of bed and sat in the bedside chair. As he sat up straight and relaxed, closed his eyes and began deep breathing, he realized he had a lot to talk about with Spirit tonight!

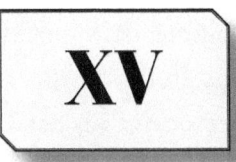

XV

The next day was a busy one for Larry. Early in the morning, someone came by with a wheelchair and took him to be x-rayed. Later his doctor, Dr. Dunniger, came by with two other doctors, and they gave Larry a thorough examination, asking him many, many questions, then looked into his eyes with a small light again. They went into the hall and talked earnestly with each other, seemed to come to a consensus of opinion, and came back and stood by his bedside, solemnly looking at him.

Dr. Dunninger began, "Larry, it seems you've made a remarkable recovery. When you were admitted to this hospital you were at the point of death, and at least one time you were dead. Now your x-rays show your fracture is completely healed, and with the exception of a small scar on your scalp there's no sign you were ever injured. My colleagues agree with me; you're healed. We're going to keep you for a few more days for observation, due to the serious nature of your injury, just to make completely sure you're going to be okay, and then you may go home!" He began to grin. "Of course, we may lose a candy stripper to a broken heart when you leave, but that's the chance we'll just have to take!"

Larry's face turned red. He was suddenly so flustered he could hardly talk. "Thank you Dr. Dunniger. I'll be glad to go home! Thank you," he stammered.

Dr. Dunniger placed his hand on Larry's shoulder. "Goodbye young man. I'll be looking in on you from time to time for the next few days, and I'll want to see you for a three-month checkup." The doctors left.

Later in the morning a nurse came in and replaced the huge bandage on his head with just a small one that looked like a head band. His hair was growing and beginning to cover where his head had been shaved surrounding the scar on the side of his head. It felt good to actually be able to scratch it when it itched!

When his Mother arrived in the evening, she told Larry the doctor had called her and told her the good news about him being healed and able to go home in a few days. She was excited! She was making plans for the kids from church to give him a party. Brother Raeburn and Sister McDougal planned to be there too. Although he could appreciate the reason she was doing it, news about the party did not really excite Larry.

"Mom, what about Dad? What's going to happen there?" Larry asked.

His Mom was quiet for a few seconds, then said seriously, with a sober look on her face, "You don't worry about that. I'll take care of him! We're gonna have a serious talk when I get home tonight. He's either going to get a new attitude and start behaving differently or he will have to leave." She turned her head away from him and he could tell she was wiping tears from her cheeks.

"To tell you the whole truth, Larry, I've already talked to a lawyer."

"Mom, I don't want to be responsible for that," Larry said.

"You're not responsible for it, Larry. That Brother Huffstutler was the one that started the whole thing off! Arthur never should have listened to the crazy stuff he had to say. Now he's just going to have to get back to his old self, that's all, or we'll lose the sixteen years we've had together." She collapsed into the room chair and put her face in her hands. She began to cry softly.

Larry knelt down beside her and put an arm around her shoulders. "It's gonna be alright, Mom. I promise. Spirit will work it out. We just have to trust in him! Like you've said before, Dad's a good man, and he'll do the right thing. He's always taken good care of us, and he won't stop now."

His Mom stopped crying and looked deep into his eyes. "Larry, you've really changed. You're all grown up and it's like it happened almost overnight. Now you're comforting me instead of me comforting you. You're acting much older than 14!" She tenderly took his face into her hands. "Larry, you said you had lots to tell me just before you collapsed. Son, what did happen to you while you were gone?"

He drew back and sat on the bed. "I do have lots to tell you, Mom, but for right now you're just going to have to trust me. There isn't time to tell you now, but I promise to tell you everything in time. I will say this. Some of the things that happened were really tough, and some of the things that happened to me were very good. A wonderful couple took care of me. If it wasn't for them I most likely would be dead.

"In spite of the bad things that happened, it all came out good. I do know this for sure; my heart is filled with the love of Spirit, and my life belongs to Him. No matter what happens my future is in his hands, so I know everything will be just fine!"

"Oh Larry, that's so good! That's the most wonderful testimony I've ever heard!" she said. "But who's this Spirit?"

Larry smiled, remembering when he had asked Luke the very same question. "That's just another word for God, Mom. You'll just have to trust me! It's almost time for your trolley, and it's the last one tonight. You'd better go."

"Well, ok, but you remember you promised to tell me everything! Good night, Larry. Love you," she said as she kissed him on the cheek, grabbed her purse, and hurried out the door.

It was his turn to collapse into the chair, take a deep breath and blow it out forcefully. Did he ever have a lot to talk over with Spirit tonight again!

XVI

The next day Larry had a lot of free time. He was taken off all medication; no shots, no pills! The only thing the nurses did was to take his temp and blood pressure every few hours and record it. He was allowed to wear his regular clothes and go wherever he chose, just as long as it was in the hospital.

One place he visited was the gift shop where he used some of his birthday money to buy stationery and a ballpoint pen. He went back to his room and began to write a letter to his Mom, and spent a couple of hours carefully composing it.

He was excited and impatient for night time! Even though there was no definite time for them to arrive, or even that they would show up, Larry felt sure Angel and Luke would be there.

About 6:30, the candy stripper, Bernadette, came to his room, smiled sweetly, and told him there was a phone call for him at the nurse's station. Puzzled, he went with her, took the phone, and hesitantly said, "Hello."

"Hello Son, this is Luke."

"Mr. Luke!" He turned his back to the nurses and tried to shield the phone, to give himself some privacy. "I've been waiting for you and Miss Angel to show up here. Where are you? What time are you gonna get here?"

"We're at Little Bit's house in Iron City, Son. I know you was expecting us, or at least I figured you would be, and I know you was expecting to leave with us, but there's a real problem. If we showed up there an' you left with us, you being jus' fourteen might cause a heap of trouble. If things didn't go jus' right we might be charged with kidnappin'! Remember, you're a minor, an' your parents still have custody of you, an' legally tell you what you can an' can't do! We decided we jus' can't take that chance, Son, even though we would love to! We're gonna truly miss you an' we hope to see you in the future. We will try to stay in touch. Now it will soon enough be time to go to the train station, an' our friend 'Little Bit' that we've been stayin' with will be takin' us there."

"But......"

"No buts, Son. We gotta go. We love you, Son, and don't you ever forget it! Bye now," and the phone went dead, then a dial tone started.

Larry was shocked, then felt devastated, and just stood there holding the phone. The candy stripper, Bernadette, carefully took it from him and hung it up. "Is there anything I can do for you, Larry, before I go home?" she shyly asked.

He stood there for a few seconds, then said, "I guess not. Thanks," slowly walked back to his room, and sank into his room chair. He sat there for about fifteen minutes, staring into space and feeling sorry for himself, then he sat straight up!

"I told them I'd go alone and find them and I will!" He tucked the letter to his Mom just under the edge of his pillow, quickly arranged his bedding, turned out his room light, cautiously peeked down the hall toward the nurse's station, and then quickly walked to the stairwell and down one flight of stairs to the first floor. Slowing down, he confidently walked out the front door.

There in front of the hospital a taxi was parked. A small man got out and asked, "Are you Larry?"

Startled, he said, "Yes sir. How did you know?"

"Luke sent me. My name's Little Bit. Luke said you might need a ride!" He opened the back door and Larry got in.

They pulled away from the curb. "Luke had a feeling you was gonna do this. Said you was stubborn, an' wanted to make sure you was safe. So he sent me to watch out for you. Me an' Luke growed up together an' he protected me lots of times from the big boys that wanted to pick on me an' bully me. You know how that can go, but nobody was bigger an' stronger than Luke! So I figure I owe him a few favors, an' I'm glad I can help him out when he needs it! If we hurry a little bit, I think we can still make it to the train station in time."

Larry settled back into his seat and Little Bit continued to talk non stop, telling him about times when Luke stood up for him when they were kids. Larry was looking out his side window and realized the scenery began to look familiar. He looked over at Little Bit and asked, "Is this the way to the train station? This looks like my old neighborhood."

Little Bit hesitated just for a second and then said, "It is your old neighborhood, Larry. Luke wanted us to pick up one more passenger. Said tell you not to worry. He has a plan!" They pulled up in front of the house next to Larry's and Little Bit turned out the lights and shut off the engine. This was a working-class neighborhood and most people were already in bed asleep so they could get up early the next morning and go to work. Little Bit said, "Luke wanted you to bring Spot. Go get him and put him in the back seat. We have to be quiet and quick now before someone calls the cops and we have all kinds of trouble!"

Larry opened the door, got out and quietly closed it. Moving quickly to the gate to the back yard, he let himself in. Spot was excitedly wagging his tail from end to end and whining softly. Larry dropped to one knee and hugged him. "We have to be quiet, Boy," he whispered. Grabbing a handful of hair on the back of Spot's neck, he led him out the gate and to the car, opened the back door and whispered, "Get in, Boy." Spot hesitated and looked up at Larry.

Larry quickly jumped into the back seat and said, "Come on in, Boy." Without hesitation Spot jumped into the back seat. Larry quietly closed the door and Little Bit cranked the car and pulled away from the curb. He turned the corner and quickly headed for the train station.

For the next couple of minutes Larry and Spot had their reunion. Spot was whining and licking his face all over and Larry was hugging his neck. When they had settled down Little Bit handed something to Larry over the back of the front seat. "Ok, here's the plan according to Luke. This is a special harness for a guide dog. They won't let just any dog on the train, but they might a guide dog. So for tonight and the rest of the trip you're a blind boy and Spot is your guide dog! Luke is wearing his doctor's coat and will be your doctor and Angel your nurse, and they're accompanying you to wherever it is you're going."

Larry sat back and his mouth dropped open. Then he began to grin. Leave it to Luke to come up with a plan like that, and it just might work! He began to put the harness on Spot. Spot had never even had a collar on and was a little confused at first, but he trusted Larry completely, and soon Larry had the harness on him. Little Bit reached back and handed Larry something else. "Here's some sunglasses, Larry. When we get to the station, you can put these on and wear 'em for the rest of the trip. It'll just add to your image as the little blind boy!" Larry sat back in the seat and grinned as he began to imagine what was coming.

Soon they arrived at the train station, and standing out front was Luke and Angel with Luke wearing his doctor's coat. Little Bit pulled the taxi to the curb and parked. He got out and opened the back door for Larry and Spot. Larry got out wearing his sunglasses and hanging on to Spot's harness. Spot was confused by his new surroundings, but Larry bent down to pet and reassure him, and he quickly settled down. Luke walked over with the back of his hand extended to Spot, and Spot sniffed it, looked up and wagged his tail. Larry reached out to touch Luke, Luke put his hand on Larry's shoulder, and Angel gave him a hug. Spot observed all this and seemed to immediately accept these new people.

"Little Bit, can't tell you how much I 'preciate your help," Luke said. "I owe you!"

"Luke, you don't owe me nothin', and I look forward to helpin' you agin sometime!" Little Bit said, sticking out his hand for a warm handshake. "You all just have a good trip now. I got to move my taxi or they'll be chasin' me off! Bye now." He got in the car and drove away.

"I already got the tickets, so we can go git on the train. It's almost time for it to be leavin'," Luke said. They walked through the station, with Angel to the right side of Larry, who was holding on to Spot's harness with his left hand, and Luke walking close to Spot's side, on out to the tracks. They walked up to a conductor standing next to a portable step platform by a train.

Luke handed him the tickets and the conductor looked them up and down. "No dogs!", he said, and handed the tickets back to Luke.

Luke didn't take the tickets and said, "I'm Dr. Luke and this is my nurse," pointing to Angel. "This young man is going to Ashland where he and his dog will get more training before he goes to private school."

The conductor said, "I've had lots of doctors on my train and you don't look like no doctor to me, especially not with those muddy boots and jeans!"

Luke hesitated just for a second as he had to think of a way around this new problem. "Mr. Conductor, I work for this boy's Daddy in a lumber camp in Wilson County. When he told me 'Go with my boy' I didn't take time to change into my traveling clothes."

Still skeptical, the conductor said, "That don't look like no seeing-eye dog I've ever seen! All the ones I've seen are German Shepherds."

Luke said, "Yeah, but the Shepherds are getting to be so expensive they're trying something new with different breeds. That's why we're going to Ashland to get more training."

The conductor looked at the tickets, hesitated, and then punched them. Handing them back to Luke, he said, "I'll be keeping an eye on you. Any trouble at all and I'm putting you off my train. Understand?"

"Yes sir, you won't have no trouble out of us!" Luke said. They started forward and Spot hesitated, obviously confused and fearful of the train. Without hesitation Luke reached down and scooped him up and bounded up the train steps. "Guess they didn't train him to trains yet. That's another reason to be going to Ashland. Nurse, help the conductor get Larry aboard," and he disappeared into the car.

The conductor guided Larry's hand to the handrail, with Angel reaching and trying to assist. It was all Larry could do not to smile as he tried to play his part.

They were soon seated. Larry and Spot across the aisle from Luke and Angel. The train almost immediately started rolling and pulled out of the station.

Angel said, "Larry, we're so glad you made it in time. I hope you understand why we had to do things like we did. You had to leave on your own. Luke and me just couldn't stand the kind of trouble we could get into if we tried to help you. What did you tell your Mother?"

Larry's expression became very serious and he hesitantly looked over at Angel. "I didn't exactly tell her about my decision to leave with you. I was afraid she would try to stop me, and she probably would have. I did leave her a long letter explaining why I am leaving, and I made her a lot of promises. I promised to call her often, and I promised to go to school and finish. If I can I'll call her tomorrow when we get to where we're going. She won't be very happy, and I'm not happy about leaving her either. I know I'll miss her lots but I just feel this is the best thing for me to do.

"Like I told her in the letter, I just can't go back to the way I was! I've changed and don't fit in there anymore!" His frustration and desperation were beginning to show in his face and in his voice.

"It's ok Larry, it's ok.. We know it will be rough on you for a long time. There will be a long period of adjustment, and we'll do all we can to help you through it," Angel softly said.

"One thing we can do is make sure you keep the promises you made to her! You'll give her a call first thing when we get to our stop in the morning. And tell her you'll send her a copy of every report card you get at school!" Luke chimed in.

"Yes sir, I understand. By the way, thanks for sending Little Bit."

"Who?" Luke grinned. "Don't have the slightest idea who you mean." He settled back into his seat and looked straight ahead, a slight satisfied grin on his face.

Larry leaned back in his seat. He reflected briefly on the difference this train ride was to the last time he left Iron City on a train, just a few months ago, and smiled. The person he was now, compared to the boy he was then, and all the experiences he'd had and survived, seemed almost unreal, like a long dream and sometimes nightmare, a strange combination of observer and participant. He glanced across the aisle at his two best friends in the world. Not only were they his best friends, but also his surrogate parents and protectors. A warm and safe feeling enveloped him. He wasn't sure where they were going and he didn't really care. He was continuing on the journey to the rest of his life and felt confident that, with the help of his friends and Spirit, he could handle anything that came along. Little did he realize how much this feeling was going to be challenged.

To be continued

LUKE'S TRUEISMS

The Bible says God is Spirit and lives in each of us. That's the Christ Spirit within us.

When we git quiet an' still and sit in the silence, Spirit can talk with us.

Every human being has a spot of the Christ Spirit and dignity in him, although many folks has it hid real good!

If we look for the good in everybody, we'll find that most people are just naturally good when they have a chance to be.

Most of the time, if somebody is being mean or evil, it comes from fear.

It's always a good thing to say. "Spirit, guide me now."

Our attitude will usually make all the difference in how somethin' turns out.

Now, if you have a problem to solve, you can pray about it 'til the cows come home, but ain't nothin' good gonna happen 'til you take some kind of action!

There's always a reason bad people are bad.

We each have to follow our own path, an' play the cards that are dealt to us.

If someone can't scare you, they can't control you.

Jesus was convinced of the dignity of man, and talked about it in his teachins.

Jesus taught love, forgiveness, compassion, the divinity of man, an' simple livin'. He didn't teach punishment.

We are the only people we can change, only us.